finding
the
gROOVE

COMPOSING A
JAZZ-SHAPED
FAITH

Finding
the
gRoove

ROBERT GELINAS

ZONDERVAN®

ZONDERVAN.com/
AUTHORTRACKER
follow your favorite authors

ZONDERVAN®

Finding the Groove
Copyright © 2009 by Robert Gelinas

This title is also available in a Zondervan audio edition. Visit www.zondervan.fm.

Requests for information should be addressed to:

Zondervan, *Grand Rapids, Michigan 49530*

Library of Congress Cataloging-in-Publication Data

Gelinas, Robert, 1969–.
    Finding the groove : composing a jazz-shaped faith / Robert Gelinas.
       p.   cm.
    Includes bibliographical references.
    ISBN 978-0-310-28252-5 (softcover)
    1. Jazz—religious aspects—Christianity. 2. Christian life. I. Title.
ML3921.8.J39G46   2009
261.5'78—dc22   2008036186

Published in association with the literary agency of Wolgemuth & Associates, Inc.

Interior design by Beth Shagene

Printed in the United States of America

---

08 09 10 11 12 13 • 22 21 20 19 18 17 16 15 14 13 12 11 10 9 8 7 6 5 4 3 2 1

For Barbara, my beloved.
After all of these years, I still can't believe
that you said "yes!"

contents

As blues-beset as life may be,
the real secret is somehow to make life swing,
to survive by staying in the groove.
Ralph Ellison

finding
the
gROOVe

setting the stage

When I was in college, I used to study for my Greek and Hebrew exams at a local jazz venue. I was fascinated as the ensemble played together, in concert with and for each other. As I watched the way the musicians supported one another, casting glances to communicate, and how each instrument complemented its neighbor—IT began to dawn on me.

One time, young and old, rich and poor, country and hip-hop, black, brown, and white, surrounded me. The band had a Latin saxophonist and a young dreadlocked brother on stand-up bass. On piano and drums two middle-aged men, one black and the other white, played together.

As the groove began, the saxophone player motioned for someone in the crowd, an elderly black man, who slowly made his way to the stage. His voice was far from perfect, but as this man sang about love gained and love lost . . .

· IT was present
he had IT
we wept because of IT

For almost two decades now, I have wondered what it is about this thing called jazz that brings so many kinds of people together. Oftentimes I listen to a saxophonist solo, and I can't help but think that there's something in this for me. When I see an eclectic ensemble allowing for fresh takes on old standards, or as I look around the sometimes smoke-filled room and see that I am sitting with all hues of skin, I sense that there is something in this for the body of Christ.

As followers of Christ I think that we have something to learn from jazz. For as I watch the way Jesus interacted with people, healing one blind man with a word and using saliva on another, I see him improvising. As I ponder how he taught, drawing on old themes in fresh ways, I see IT in Jesus. I see Jesus in IT.

* * *

A jazz-shaped faith is worth pursuing because it balances freedom with boundaries, the individual with the group, and traditions with the pursuit of what might be. I have discovered in jazz a way of thinking, living, communicating—a way of being ... a groove. Not a rut, but rather a set of factors that converge, creating a place to settle in and space to be.

Jazz is not the solution to all of the flaws of our faith. Rather it is a way for you and me to experience the gospel—the coming of the kingdom of God—in spite of and because of our deficiencies. The revolutionary movement of Jesus crosses racial, cultural, socioeconomic, denominational, and generational divides, and in the midst of our "franchise" approach to life and faith there is a crying need for something old and new, fresh and yet not novel—something that allows for our weaknesses and strengths. A groove that gives new life to the Scriptures, church, and the way we view community. I often wonder what it would look like if we composed a jazz-shaped Christianity.

What if there was a way for Christians to live with the tensions of our faith and to embrace their beauty?

What if you and I experienced church like a jazz ensemble (listening to the beat of the image of God in each of us) and community meant that you and I felt connected, not only to those we can see, but also with those who *have followed* (in past generations) and *have yet* (in future generations) *to follow* Jesus?

What if there is another way to know the Scriptures? What if we experienced the word of God as a song that sets us free to compose, a melody that has room for our voice to join in with the ancients?

What if every moment of life with Jesus is pregnant

with promise, containing the potential to be a one-of-a-kind masterpiece?

What if so much of what has gone wrong with America has also produced something that is right and good, allowing for us to live and love with soul because we understand why caged birds sing?

What if we could find the groove and in the process live in IT?

These are the questions I have been asking in the hope of composing a jazz-shaped faith that will lead me closer to the kingdom of God in our midst.

Something Is Out of Sync

This whole issue is personal for me. At times my faith gets out of sync. I have moments when the Scriptures fail to intrigue or inspire. Times when I long for the desire of the psalmist to meditate on them day and night, for them to be food for my soul, for the word to be alive, piercing, and real. At times, it feels as if something is missing. I have an unshakable sense that something is off in the way we pray, read our Bibles, and worship. The barriers of race, class, generation, and denomination continue to keep us apart, and we are not sure of the last time we felt that those in the pew next to us were truly brothers and sisters, let alone those who attend other churches.

I love the church. I believe in it so much that I have given my life to it, but my eyes are wide open: "No institution has accomplished so much for good in this world; none has fallen so short of its calling!"[1] We have to come to grips with the paradoxical truth that "eleven o'clock Sunday may be the most segregated hour of the week as far as any particular parish goes, but it is the most integrated hour of the week as far as the kingdom goes."[2] Something is out of sync. Do you sense it? Do you feel the wobble in the wheel? How can it be that we are alive during one of the greatest moves of the Holy Spirit in history and yet most of us don't even know? We marvel as we read that three thousand people came into the kingdom in Acts 2, yet many estimate that around the world today, some three thousand people *an hour* are coming to know this Jesus whom we serve! Just not here in America.[3]

My undergraduate degree is in biblical studies, and at seminary I focused on missiology (the study of the mission of the church). My first degree was concerned with what the Scriptures say; the latter focused on how we communicate and live the faith in the various cultures of the world. I never felt called to go to "the mission field" but rather to live in my own country, among my own people, with "missionary eyes."

Contextualization is the process of taking the truths of Christianity in one hand and a given culture in the other, and then discerning what is compatible with the gospel and what needs redemption. For example, is drinking wine, wearing pants, or the practice of some tribes to initiate their boys into manhood by sending them on a lion hunt in line with the ways of Jesus? Many a missionary has struggled with this process because we are not neutral, unbiased observers. We bring our own culture to the faith and often end up trying to make people over in our image. However, there are "eureka moments" when one realizes that something exists in a culture that gives unique form to how the faith can be understood and lived out. Like when Paul was in Athens.[4]

As the apostle walked the streets, he searched for a place of connection. He wondered how to explain the good news to these erudite philosophical people. He was Jewish, but the Athenians were Greek. He could have taught them to be Jewish first and then to follow Jesus, but God does not require that we shed our culture to know him. Therefore, Paul looked to see if there was something in their culture that would provide a starting point. He happened upon an altar ascribed to an "unknown God." This altar was unique to them, and Paul brilliantly utilized it as a means to deliver the gospel of the kingdom. This altar was not a Christian image, but it could be redeemed for Christ and his purposes.

What if we do what Paul did? What if we do the work of a missionary right here in our own backyard? When I look at our history and culture with "missionary eyes," I see something indigenous that *we have yet to fully explore and apply to our faith*. Embedded in our way of life is something that has shown the ability to produce creativity, diversity, community, innovation, and depth. Moreover, it originated in the church, though the church abandoned it, rejected it, and has all but forgotten that it exists. What is it? It's jazz.

Discovering it caused me to rethink my beliefs. Not what I believe but how I believe what I believe. Seeking an understanding of jazz has led me to experience our mysterious God and the community to which he calls us in ways that have surprised me. Jazz has given me a new desire to truly know God's word and Christ's incarnation, life, death, and resurrection. A jazz-shaped faith has even led me to

> Jazz music celebrates life — human life. The range of it. The absurdity of it. The ignorance of it. The greatness of it. The intelligence of it. The sexuality of it. The profundity of it.
> **Wynton Marsalis, jazz musician**

strive to embrace suffering for all it has to offer and to refuse to waste temptation. It has changed the way I see people, or shall I say, I have begun to not just see people but to hear them and the song of God in their lives.

Before all of that, though, I needed to understand what it was. Those late-night questions, with college books in my hands and a jazz ensemble grooving in the background, set the stage for my journey of composition. What I discovered is that Ralph Ellison was on to something when he said that all of American life is "jazz shaped." By that, he meant that jazz is *more* than music, and therein lies the hope of a composed and composing life with God—culminating in a jazz-shaped faith.

more than music

You don't need to be a musician to possess a jazz-shaped faith. I love jazz. I listen to it, read about it, and connect with it. However, I am not a musician. I cannot read music or even play an instrument. It's certainly not for lack of trying. I have toyed with the trumpet and experimented with the saxophone. I even have a piano sitting in my office. After seven years of guitar lessons, all I have to show for it is the ability to play "Yankee Doodle" on demand. The wonderful thing about composing a jazz-shaped faith is that musical ability is not necessary, because jazz is *more than music*.

Composing a jazz-shaped faith meant that I had to expand my conception of what jazz is. Defining jazz is complicated, in part, because of its relative youth. Jazz came into being barely over a century ago. Historically speaking, jazz is merely an awkward adolescent trying to figure out what it is going to be when it grows up. We do not even know where the word *jazz* comes from, except that it evolved from the earlier—probably derogatory—spelling *jass*. (When some bigoted people saw former slaves playing and dancing to this new style of music, they said something to the effect of, "Look at those jackasses." "Jackass" was shortened to "jass" and eventually slurred into "jazz.")[1]

Nonetheless, what I found is that there has been no shortage of definitions—and most of them are *nonmusical*. Whitney Balliett said that jazz is "the sound of surprise."[2] Ray Charles reasoned that jazz was "Genius + Soul."[3] Ralph Ellison declared that jazz was an institution of America, equal to the Constitution and the Bill of Rights.[4]

Jazz—an institution?

Perhaps it is. After all, the Latin root for *institution* is *statuer*, which means "to put in place" or "to stand."[5] And in some sense that's what jazz is to me—a place to be, a place from which I can see and hear, be seen and heard.

> Jazz is Jazz
>
> Louis Armstrong, jazz trumpeter and singer

Ultimately, what I have come to believe is that jazz is a window into America's soul. When you watch a jazz ensemble jam together, you are witnessing the retelling of a good chunk of American history—an "audible history," so to speak—for jazz did not exist before this country came into being. Rather, it's the product of one of America's original sins. To talk about jazz is to talk about race and the unique struggle that this new invention of classifying people by skin color wrought. Pain gave way to the blues, and the blues gave way to jazz—they are all connected.

Jazz was born of the desire for freedom, independence, and autonomy within the bounds and bonds of America. The beautiful thing is that in the process, it was able to accomplish something that nothing else had. At a time when the Ku Klux Klan was on the rise, lynchings were commonplace, and segregation separated human beings—even according to their bathroom habits—something remarkable was happening: blacks and whites were coming together in the same room to play and listen to jazz, oftentimes as equals!

This became all too clear when I watched the epic documentary *Jazz: A Film by Ken Burns*, which tells of the beginnings and growth of jazz as music.[6] Burns does a masterful job of telling the jazz story and exploring the importance of key individuals. His series is full of vintage photos and recordings. He also includes a plethora of interviews in which you can hear varying points of view from critics and musicians alike. My favorite definition of jazz comes from Geoffrey Ward and Ken Burns's monumental accompanying book *Jazz: A History of America's Music*:

The history of jazz turns out to be much more than a study of this extraordinary American music. Jazz has been a prism through which so much of American history can be seen — a curious and unusually objective witness to the twentieth century. And so jazz necessarily becomes a story about race and race relations and prejudice, about minstrelsy and Jim Crow, lynching and civil rights.... Our study of jazz offers the explosive hypothesis that *those who have had the peculiar experience of being unfree in a free land* [emphasis mine] might actually be at the center of our history.[7]

"Unfree in a free land." I'll never forget when I heard those words. Immediately I thought of how utterly absurd the life of a slave in America was. Kidnapped from your homeland, packed into the belly of a ship, chained down so that you could not even sit up, let alone use the restroom in a sanitary manner. In the land ahead you faced "de-Africanization," that is, the wholesale assault on your body, culture, and mind. "Not allowed to be Africans, and ... not accepted as Americans."[8] Imagine for a moment that you were "fortunate" to have survived the trek across the Atlantic, and as you step off the ship you are able to ask, "Where am I?" The response you receive: "You are in America. The land of liberty." What immeasurable grief that would have created in your life as you stood there with shackles on your wrists and ankles!

"Unfree in a free land."

This experience "created" a new people group, a new tribe that had not existed before coming to this country. This group of people would wrestle for centuries with what it means to be in chains in the land of the free. The "unfree in a free land" coexisted with people experiencing unprecedented liberty. This existential tension stirred up yearnings and aspiration for certain God-given unalienable rights of life, liberty, and the pursuit of happiness. These yearnings gave rise to the blues, and blues gave birth to this music of freedom within boundaries, becoming within the constraints of the song and ensemble—this jazz.

> [Jazz] is the music of a people who have long had to live within a society more determinatively defined by others, and know how to make do with limits and material that were not self-chosen.
>
> **Rodney Clapp, *Border Crossings***

I have to admit that as an African-American I have a visceral connection with jazz. It speaks to me. I cannot listen to Louis Armstrong, Nina Simone, or Miles Davis without simultaneously rehearsing in my mind the history that made jazz not only possible but necessary. As someone who spent much of my early life struggling with identity, trying to figure out what it means to be an African-American, a hyphenated person, jazz helps me with the tension. Am I both/and, either/or, neither—why does it even matter? Jazz serves as a vista from which I can see and wrestle with the options, for it is a product of dilemmas such as these. Yet even if you are not an African-American, you will discover that one of the unique surprises that comes with understanding jazz is how it helps all of us see our history and other people from a different vantage point. Jazz provides a safe space to think about our country, race, and culture. That being said, the reason I keep returning to jazz is because it helps me to follow Jesus.

I think of Joseph sold by his own brothers into slavery. He spent years in prison for a crime he did not commit, and he lost decades of life that could have been spent with his father, who loved him. Yet Joseph said to his cowering brothers, "You intended to harm me, but God intended it for good to accomplish what is now being done, the saving of many lives."[9] That's how I feel about jazz. I never would have picked the conditions that brought it into being, but I'm sure grateful that it exists. Because we now have at our disposal indispensable tools wrought out of suffering, which can show us new ways of following our Suffering Servant.

I like jazz in music, but I love jazz in my faith. As lead pastor (and resident jazz theologian) of Colorado

Community Church, I have seen jazz at work. We are an interdenominational, intergenerational, multi-cultural, multicampus mission in the Denver metro area. Each week, I see the people of God living in unity and serving sacrificially, regardless of skin color. I see young and old, rich and poor, holding hands in worship. And in moments like these, I am grateful for the gospel. I am grateful for jazz. I am grateful for having discovered the gospel in jazz!

key notes

Around midnight, after a late-night study session at the jazz club, I began packing up my books so I could catch the bus. I was sitting next to the stage, and I heard someone above me ask, "What are you doing?"

I looked up and saw the percussionist leaning over the rail. "What are you doing?" he repeated. "Every time you come in here, I'm up on stage trying to play my best, and you have your nose in a book. Why is that?" I explained to him that I was in college and that I enjoyed studying while listening to his music.

This was my chance to gain insight. I told him that I was intrigued by jazz and that I studied at the jazz club, of all places, because I was trying to figure out what he was doing. I shared with him my call to serve God and that what he was doing on the stage seemed as though it could connect with all of the theology I was studying. I told him that I was trying to figure it out, but I didn't understand the code. This was the beginning of many conversations in which I shared with him about the things of God and he shared with me about the things of jazz. What I learned is that there are three basic concepts, *key notes* if you will, that unlock jazz: syncopation, improvisation, and call-and-response.

Jazz is more than music, though music is a good place to start. That's why listening to jazz can be helpful when it comes to composing a jazz-shaped faith. I prefer the jazz greats such as Duke Ellington, John Coltrane, Miles Davis, and Sarah Vaughn. When I teach about these concepts, I like to do so with a full jazz ensemble behind me. Talented and practiced musicians are a living metaphor, and if we can learn to see these key notes in music, then we can translate them into our faith. You may or may not enjoy jazz music, and that's fine. My goal is not to persuade you to program your car stereo to local jazz stations or to fill your iPod with jazz classics (though that would not be a bad thing). A jazz-shaped faith is not about liking the music or introducing smooth jazz versions of hymns into our worship services. Rather, it is about understanding and incorporating the essence of jazz into the way we follow Jesus. I've learned from personal experience that jazz, as music, is a good place to start when it comes to understanding and learning to recognize the basic elements. If we can learn to hear and see it in music, we can then apply the key notes to our faith.

Jazz is most accessible in the realm of instruments, sounds, 4/4 time, and musicians who call themselves "cats." Music is an easy way to discover the basics of this way of being in and seeing the world.

It Don't Mean a Thing ...

Jazz swings. That is, it picks up momentum, presses forward, and searches for what is to come. *Syncopation* is the technique that creates this characteristic. Simply put, syncopation is accenting the offbeat. My newfound jazz friend was a percussionist, so this was the first thing he taught me.

Sitting at a table he said, "Take your right hand and tap it, saying,

'One ... two ... three ... four.'"

Then he had me add my left hand between the beats to accent the offbeat, tapping and saying,

"One ... and ...

two ... and ...

three ... and ... four."

That's syncopation in its most basic form. Other styles of music make use of this technique, but as one person has said, "Jazz is syncopation gone mad."

Syncopation is what makes jazz swing, and swing is what causes you to want to move, to dance, to sit with your eyes closed and take on the cool head nod in the corner. Syncopation is what makes the music feel alive. All because of the accent on the offbeat. You accent that which was always there but hasn't been heard. Syncopation is not limited to musicians; it just requires an eye and ear for that which goes unnoticed and unheard in life.

Jesus was a master at noticing the unnoticed. I can't help but think of the crowd surrounding him as he followed the worried father of a twelve-year-old girl. Jesus was fully aware of the "main beats," but he also accented the "offbeats."

"Who touched me?" Jesus said. The question made no sense to the disciples. Many people in the crowd were pushing and pressing on him. How could they identify who had touched him? Yet Jesus "heard" something and noticed the unnoticed. While everyone was focused on a twelve-year-old girl who was dying, Jesus felt the touch of a woman who had been bleeding for twelve years, and he accented the offbeat, allowing everyone to see what God was doing in her life as well.[1] When we learn the art of syncopation, our awareness of each moment increases. We see what is evident while we search for that which is present, though unnoticed.

> Don't play what's there, play what's not there.
>
> Miles Davis, jazz musician

We can even syncopate the Scriptures. There is so

much in our Bibles that is yet to be discovered in the offbeats. I am not talking about finding hidden meaning but meaning often missed because of where we choose to place the emphasis.

Duke Ellington said it best: "It don't mean a thing if it ain't got that swing."

Never the Same Old Song

Improvisation is what allows jazz to exist in a continual state of renewal. In jazz, the same old song seems like a new song every time it is performed because it is a music of traditions and freedom. Much of the fun comes from hearing how new artists will take old standards and make them fresh as they add their own voices.

As with syncopation, it's not that other forms of music do not make use of this skill—they do. But in jazz, improvisation is expected. When jazz musicians take the stage, they are there, in part, to take the risk of composing in the moment—improvisation.

The word *improvisation* derives from the Latin *im* and *provisus*, meaning "not provided" or "not foreseen." Improvisation is the willingness to live within the bounds of the past and yet to search for the future at the same time. Improvisation is the desire to make something new out of something old. It is the craving to respect tradition while at the same time leaving one's own mark. Improvisation is having a plan and yet not being incarcerated by the plan. It is experienced in being open to letting the people around you, whether they are in the band or spectators in the audience, have input into and impact on what you are creating.

> Jazz is music that's never played the same way once.
>
> **Louis Armstrong, jazz trumpeter and singer**

Wynton Marsalis is the artistic director of jazz at the Lincoln Center for the Performing Arts in New York City. He's earned a Pulitzer Prize, written several books, and plays a mean trumpet. On a Tuesday evening late in August 2001 at the Village Vanguard in Greenwich Village, he was playing "I Don't Stand a Ghost of a Chance with You" on his trumpet without accompaniment. As he neared the end of the song, the sound of a cell phone intruded into the drama of the moment. A jazz critic in the audience scrawled on a sheet of notepaper, "MAGIC, RUINED," and people began to chatter. Marsalis improvised. He played the notes of the cell phone ring tone—slow, fast, and in different keys—and when all ears were back on him, he seamlessly transitioned the silly cell phone tune back to the ballad and finished the song. In the words of the jazz critic, "The ovation was tremendous."[2]

Improvisation is about adventure, play, and experimentation. It is about being so familiar with one's instrument of choice, the song, and the essentials that we can trust ourselves to search for the unseen—for what the moment is presenting. When we incorporate improvisation into our faith, freedom follows (for jazz is all about freedom!). Not freedom for freedom's sake. Rather, freedom within and freedom that results from the good and right standards of our God. Improvisation will keep us from just copying others spiritually and set us free to play a little.

Do you think that God composes in the moment? For sure, he knows all things. There are no particles of space dust beyond his gaze, nor is there a piece of information stored on some hard drive that is outside of his awareness. God knows all things—past, present, and future; however, I do not think that this keeps him from having some fun and allowing us to influence his compositions. He seems very open to interaction with us. He allows us to have input and seems open to cooperating with us on the future. We only need to read of God's interactions with Abraham, who pleads for Sodom; with Moses, who negotiates with God after the golden calf incident; or with Jonah, who runs in the opposite direction to avoid God's call, to discover that God is creatively cooperating with us.[3] Jesus gave a whole new meaning to what it means to live a "composed" life as he sent his disciples out and told them that the Spirit would give them what to say in the moment.[4]

Can I Get an Amen?

Jazz was conceived, birthed, and incubated in the slave church, in which *call-and-response* was a way of life. Call-and-response was and is a way for everybody to be involved in the preaching event. It was also a way to support the preacher. Just imagine a group of Christ-following slaves gathered at night, crying out to God. Among them is an illiterate man who feels called to preach. As he stands up, his fellow slaves want him to know that he is not up there alone.

Preacher calls: "I am here tonight to speak to you about forgiveness."

Congregation responds: "Help him, Jesus!"

When he struggles with a concept, they say, "Make it plain."

When he makes it plain, they encourage him by responding with affirmations of applause and "Amen!"

The preacher calls and congregation responds; horn calls and piano responds. Call-and-response makes listening to jazz music an adventure as you begin to hear the instruments as voices calling to each other and engaging in conversation.

Jazz, Jazz Everywhere

Once I became familiar with these key notes, I began
to see jazz everywhere, for all of American life is jazz
shaped, and jazz is more than music. Additionally, I
began to experiment with them in everyday life and
found others in history who had done the same. For
example, when Langston Hughes wrote the following
words in his poem "Harlem: A Dream Deferred," he
was doing jazz:

> *What happens to a dream deferred?*
>
> *Does it dry up*
> *like a raisin in the sun?*
> *Or fester like a sore—*
> *And then run?*
> *Does it stink like rotten meat?*
> *Or crust and sugar over—*
> *like a syrupy sweet?*
>
> *Maybe it just sags*
> *like a heavy load.*
>
> *Or does it explode?*[5]

Hughes was not the first of the jazz poets, but he is
definitely one of the most notable. These poets began
by including references to the music and musicians in
their prose. Then they quickly embarked on apply-
ing what they saw the musicians doing on stage and

translated it into their verse. Making use of syncopation, repetition, and the blues, they gave birth to a new way of doing poetry—poetry in jazz.

Langston Hughes called and Ralph Ellison responded.

Ellison was a trumpeter and lifelong lover of jazz. He not only asserted that American life is "jazz shaped," he sought to demonstrate it when he wrote the great American novel *Invisible Man*. Ellison, a longtime jazz critic, moved from writing about jazz to writing in jazz.

He was responding to the poetic question of his friend Langston: *What happens to a dream deferred?*

He hints at this in the prologue to his novel when the main character seeks to light his darkness by illuminating it with 1,369 lightbulbs. The number is a coded tribute to the year 1936—the year Ellison moved to New York City during the Harlem Renaissance and met Langston Hughes.

Ellison's work is a jazzlike response to Langston's call: What happens to the American Dream when it is deferred for a group of people? (The answer, by the end of *Invisible Man*, is a resounding "yes—it explodes!")

He didn't stop there. He wanted to see if he could write a whole novel in jazz. Could he syncopate and improvise with the written word. Ellison demonstrates that jazz is more than music. Ellison is an essential link for me for believing in the possibility of a jazz-shaped Christianity. What he demonstrated was that while jazz is mainly known as music, jazz is *more than music.*

Ellison even writes a trumpet solo in words that carries through the novel. He accomplishes this with three words in *Invisible Man*: red, white, and blue. In his prologue, he plays these three colors as a chord by first describing a dessert and then a tattoo. Once he thinks you are following, he begins to improvise. The joy of the novel is trying to figure out how he is going to play these notes. Trying to figure out the symbolisms of the colors keeps us actively engaged. Does the color red represent blood or Native Americans? Does white only represent Caucasian people? And does the color blue mean to be black? That is, does it represent the slaves who had been beaten black-and-blue? One thing is for sure: it represents the pain that brought the blues about. Reading *Invisible Man* is like listening to a trumpet take a solo, and you wait on the edge of your seat wondering how he is going to pull it all together and find his way back.

When I first saw this, my mind was spinning—certainly because of the brilliance of the man and the intricacy of his writing, but, more important, because he, along with Hughes, had shown us that jazz is more than music. His novel *Invisible Man* is a jazz text. As a jazz musician, he decided to see if jazz could exist in another medium—eureka!

If jazz is more than music, then the jazz-shaping possibilities are endless.

Music has found form in jazz. Poetry discovered existence in jazz. Literature made the leap and found expression in jazz. What would it look like to believe in jazz? To express our faith in jazz? To convey the glorious gospel in jazz? The gospel! That is ultimately what this is about. The good news of that radical carpenter from Nazareth whose message transforms people, homes, families, neighborhoods, and all of creation from the inside out. The coming of the kingdom of God, announced and inaugurated by Jesus on the cross for all who would believe. This is about what could happen if we respond to the call of a love supreme in all of its improvised and syncopated glory.

CHAPTER 4

CREATIVE TENSION

*What if there was a way for Christians
to live with the tensions of our faith
and to embrace their beauty?*

Our faith is full of tension. I remember when I was
trying to figure out whether or not we have free will.
Did I choose God, or did God choose me? I would
argue with people about these concepts, taking different sides in different debates because I couldn't figure out which one I actually believed. Then one day
I drove to a monastic retreat center, rented a room,
and locked myself in with my Bible. I literally read all
day and all night, with special focus on the Gospels. I
finally had the answer. Did I choose God, or did God
choose me? The answer: Yes!

Some of the tensions are intellectual; others are
more personal. As a pastor I am most passionate about

people discovering their calling. I love to tell people about how God has designs on their lives and that there are things in this world that only they can do. I believe that this calling is crucial to our identity and that all that we are should be organized around it. Yet if I'm honest, I really don't know who I am. When I go on vacation, I spend most of my time asking God who I am and what he has made me to do. I deeply desire to know my calling and pursue it with passion. I prayerfully journal through the options. God, who am I? Am I a pastor? Preacher? Writer? Communicator? Each time I go through this exercise, I end up in the same place. I don't know who I am, but I do know whose I am. I am God's. I am my wife's husband. I am my children's father. Those answers are usually enough to give me peace. And I live with the tension — that I am called to tell others that they are called, yet I don't know precisely what my calling is. A jazz-shaped faith needs to be content with tension and paradox, even when it is close to home.

Talkin' 'Trane

When John Coltrane took up the saxophone in his midteens, he showed an immediate aptitude for improvisation. As his skills improved, the sheer speed at which he played his instrument was enough to draw attention to this man. Few people in his hometown of Hamlet, North Carolina, could have imagined how his musical stylings would impact the jazz world. Yet, there's much more to Coltrane than his music, and if you read any biography about him, you will discover that significant attention is given to his spirituality as well. So, to talk 'Trane is to

recognize not only his musical talent but his soul;

see both the tension that his deep struggles with substance abuse brought to his life and the divine deliverance that came his way;

understand how his spiritual seeking and music making were interconnected;

listen not only to what he played but why he played the way he did;

lament the fact that we in our own lives don't allow God's overtures to truly transform us

Musically, Coltrane was a genius and a trendsetter. Practicing hours a day, he developed an unprecedented speed that awed all who heard. But why? What drove him to play the way he did? What pushed him to play scales at such ear-boggling, manic speed? By doing so,

Coltrane was on the cusp of changing the way jazz was played by removing the melody line as the core of the song and making sure that each artist in the ensemble had the opportunity—and the time—to do their thing. But that's only part of the story.

Though Coltrane was reared in his grandfather's church, alcohol and drugs became a part of his young adult life. Playing gigs in nightclubs gave Coltrane ready access to these substances. Gradually, his addictions became his deities, and he eventually moved in with his mother, playing less and abusing more. The many substances in his system produced much of the frenzy that he displayed on his instrument.

The year 1957 is the key to understanding Coltrane's paradoxical life. During that year he had an experience that was his defining moment as a man *and* a musician. It would change the very way he stood before a crowd, played a song, and approached life itself. We must first understand this profound experience in order to appreciate his music and—even more so—to see what jazz-shaped contribution he might make to our faith. Simply put, it was in 1957 that John Coltrane said he heard the sound of God.

One day, with the support of his wife and mother he sought the sanctuary of his room and began praying, seeking God's help to withstand the pain of the withdrawals. The presence of God and water sustained him. Four days later, he emerged a changed man, for—according to him—God had met him in a most unusual way. It was a sound, a droning resonance, a reverberation, unlike anything he had ever heard.

To truly "hear" Coltrane we must know what happened to him in that room. "It was so beautiful," he told his wife as he hopelessly tried to reproduce it on a piano. This sound transformed Coltrane into the "Soul Trane" and launched a search that would last for the rest of his life.

After that year, the titles of his songs began to make divine references that hinted at his spiritual seeking. The main difference, however, was in the speed at which he played. He still possessed the skills to play with the quickness for which he was renowned, but his reason for playing changed so that he became more methodical and measured. He would stand before audiences and solo for thirty minutes or more—slowly ... searching ... listening for the sound of God as he performed. He came to believe that if he could play that sound for others, then they, too, could experience what he had experienced during those four days in his bedroom. If you've had an experience with God that was so personal and so utterly amazing that you couldn't find words to describe it, then you can understand what Coltrane was going through. We can only imagine that Lazarus was a bit different after his four days in the grave as well.[1]

What was 'Trane doing? He was searching for that sound of God, that resonance and reverberation that served as the sound track to his lowest—yet most meaningful—moment in life. He was hunting that magnificent murmur, that melody, that met him when he was at his weakest and yet somehow becoming his strongest. He deeply desired for the sound of God to play through him as a witness to his audiences. When you listen to Coltrane's music, the question is not "Do you like what he is playing?" but "Can you hear why he is playing?"

He never found the sound again.

That's jazz

        searching

            yearning

                unresolved tensions

I am captivated by Coltrane's knowledge of the sound and his inability to find it again because what it produced in this man's life I've felt in my own life: tension—more specifically, *creative* tension.

The curious paradox of this musician's life is that he searched for something he knew existed, and yet he couldn't find it again, despite his remarkable talent. The contradiction of this man is that with his saxophone, he made sounds that crowds applauded, but he couldn't produce the one sound he was trying to play. Even so, this tension produced one of the greatest albums of all time, *A Love Supreme*, in which Coltrane faces his inability and simultaneously shows us that we can use tension to lead us to places with God we never would have gone if all of the tension of our faith were to be resolved.

Describing God

What words do you use to describe God? Many come to mind:

>   awesome
>   omnipotent
>   omniscient
>   loving
>   merciful
>   kind
>   big
>   good
>   wise

Surprisingly, one of the first things that God revealed about himself rarely makes our top five: God is creative—the most creative being in the universe! The Bible begins with God creating.[2] Imagine the sound of God's voice when he spoke—and all that is came to be. Was his voice commanding and booming, or playful and giddy? Was the sound a reverberation, or a droning resonance? In The Chronicles of Narnia, C. S. Lewis envisioned in his allegorized version of creation that God sang the world into existence.[3] Think about it: God called and creation responded; he spoke and *nothing* obeyed.

God is the most creative being in the universe.

In the opening pages of Scripture God's hands are in the clay, sculpting Adam into being and then carving Eve into existence. It appears that the Godhead works in concert during the creative process. The Father provides the raw materials, the Holy Spirit hovers in foremanlike fashion, and Jesus fashions, forms, and sustains.[4] The psalmist says that while we were in our mother's womb, God took grandmotherly care and "knit" us together.[5]

The apostle Paul describes God's creative process this way: "For we are God's workmanship, created in Christ Jesus to do good works, which God prepared in advance for us to do."[6] *Workmanship* is the Greek word *poiēma*. This is where we get our English word *poem*. What an amazing thought to think of oneself as a poem of God. How humbling to imagine God sitting down with paper and pencil and laboring over each verse of our lives. To the Greeks the word *poiēma* carried with it the connotation of "fabric" or "material." This works well with the next phrase—"created in Christ Jesus." It is as if Jesus was the workshop in which God fabricated us into being. However you parse it, this is creative talk through and through.

Creativity should be one of the first things that come to our minds when we think of God, which raises the questions, "What about me? What about us? Is creativity a word that could be used to describe most Christians?" At best, we might use words such as *passionate, kind, sincere, forgiving*; at worst, *judgmental, overbearing, close-minded*.

If Christ's redemptive work was, in part, intended to restore the image of God in us and if creativity is central to God's being, then creativity should become more and more a part of who we are. After all, Adam's first job of naming the animals is a pretty good hint that God thought humans had the potential to follow in his creative footsteps.

Or think about what it means to be under the influence of the Spirit. The first mention in the Bible of the Holy Spirit's empowering someone is for the purpose of creativity:

Then the LORD said to Moses, "See, I have chosen Bezalel son of Uri, the son of Hur, of the tribe of Judah, and I have filled him with the Spirit of God, with skill, ability and knowledge in all kinds of crafts—to make artistic designs for work in gold, silver and bronze, to cut and set stones, to work in wood, and to engage in all kinds of craftsmanship."[7]

Though human beings are incredibly creative, many have not carried this God-inspired creativity into our living out what it means to be the church, into our experiences of growing in our practice of prayer and Scripture reading. All too often, we do not follow in the imaginative and innovative ways of God when it comes to issues of faith. As a result, too much of Christianity today is generic and copycat in nature. Instead of displaying ingenuity, we have become reactionary to whatever pop culture is doing. You can almost count on the fact that there will be a Christian version of whatever tops the secular music charts. This is not inherently wrong, but it lacks originality—something our Creator has in abundance.

How is it that we who serve the most creative being in the universe have made following him so predictable, boring, and rut filled? What if we are to be constantly co-engaged in the creative works of God?

In my view, our lack of creativity is having detrimental effects in two vital areas of our faith—*our walk with God* (spirituality) and *our joining in to help others walk with God* (evangelism).

Our Walk with God

How is it that we allow the bread of life to grow stale and the living water stagnant? Why do prayer and Bible reading often feel more like duty than delight? Could it be the way we approach our time with our God?

For years, the time I spent with God could be reduced to two words: quiet time.

How exciting does that sound? Are those the words you would use for spending time with the most creative being in the universe? Don't get me wrong—I absolutely believe in the disciplines of solitude and silence. In our world of clocks and schedules, cell phones and PDAs, we need to have regular retreats that afford us the opportunity to be still and know that he is God.[8]

That said, think about a creative person like Robin Williams. Now, if I were to say that you were going to spend a half hour a day with this creative genius, would you envision it as "quiet time"? When Adam and Eve looked at their sundials and saw that it was time for their daily walk with God, I don't think they were looking forward to quiet time. They were on the edge of their seats. What is he going to say today? What is he going to show us today? Maybe today he'll explain the platypus!

Now, if you don't see yourself as a creative person,

don't let this intimidate you. I am not talking about everyone signing up to take art classes at the local community college. The point is not to put undue pressure on our times with God because we're feeling as though we need to mix things up. This is about God more than about us. I hope each of us can discover how God is creatively seeking us and then respond to him in a way that will feel very natural.

How We Help Others Walk with God

Think about the last few times you shared the gospel with someone. Did you follow the same pattern each time? Evangelism has to do with proclaiming the good news. But in America, the land of consumerism, we have reduced the majestic message of God to a sales pitch. If you want to sell a product, there is a predictable formula to follow. First, you have to convince a person that they have a specific need. Once they are convinced, then they are ready to hear how your product will address that need and lead to a better life. For example, you have a headache—so buy this aspirin, and you'll feel better. This is what we have turned evangelism into: "I see that your life is falling apart—so buy this product [Jesus], and your life will be better."

I want to learn how to tell people about the kingdom of God the way Jesus did.

Nicodemus came to Jesus under the cloak of night. "What if I've lived a good life but I'm on the wrong path?" he wonders. Jesus looks him in the eye and tells him that if he really wants the kingdom, then he must be "born again."[9] Nicodemus was most likely an elderly man nearing the end of his life and wishing he could start over, now that he knows what he knows. The offer to be "born again" was the perfect way to speak good news into his life. To an old man, being born again is good news. (Isn't it interesting that Jesus only told someone to be "born again" this one time, yet the phrase has become the norm for many Christians?)

> Anyone can make the simple complicated. Creativity is making the complicated simple.
>
> **Charles Mingus, jazz musician and composer**

Jesus had innumerable ways of communicating the good news to people. He creatively tailored his message to the person. For the woman who drew water from a shallow well in the middle of the day, he offered "living water"; to a thief experiencing the hell of the cross, he spoke of paradise, and to those looking for miraculous signs, he spoke of the sign of Jonah.[10]

The different ways Jesus communicated the gospel

were first pointed out to me in a series of conversations I had with author and professor Carl Ellis. He called the different metaphors and approaches "salvific paradigms" (that is, models of salvation). He told me that he believed more people would respond to the good news if we took the time to understand how it was good news to *them*. More people would listen if you and I were to follow the creative lead of Jesus. Instead, Ellis said, we are satisfied to live on what he called "theological welfare," relying on the creative spiritual thinking of others.

What if we were more creative in how we told people about the kingdom of God? What if we were able to respond to what God is doing in someone's life the way Jesus did—improvisationally—by presenting the good news in a way that is truly good news to that person? What if there is a salvific paradigm for *each person* in the world? Wouldn't it be like our God to have a unique way to invite each of his children into his family? I surely wouldn't put it past the most creative being in the universe.

A Surprising Source for Creativity

Creativity is essential to jazz. Improvisation requires it. Jazz is not about copying but about *creating*—and creating not just one time but *every time*.

Improvisation is about playfulness and curiosity, experimentation and adventure. Likewise, syncopation is asking, "What if?" and then having the courage to find out.

I remember watching a performance by saxophonist Nelson Rangell. Halfway through a song he began to play one note over and over. He played it fast and slow, in short bursts and long. He, in the moment, decided to search for the unknown and improvise. As I listened, I became amazed at the variety of ways in which one note could be played. It was a fun moment.

But Nelson kept playing that one note, and I began to wonder: How long is he going to do that? Do I like what he is doing? Is he ever going to stop?

It is here that jazz can help us.

In jazz, many elements go into producing the context for creativity, but one rises above the rest. We are prone to avoiding it, but if we are going to compose a jazz-shaped faith, we need to be comfortable with its presence. Even

> I'm going to give you one note today. See how many ways you can play that note — growl it, smear it, flat it, sharp it, do anything you want to it. That's how you express your feelings in this music. It's like talking.
>
> **Sidney Bechet, jazz musician and composer, to fellow musician Richard Hadlock**

more, we need to *embrace* it so that we can reap its benefits.

Tension.

Jazz finds creativity in the midst of the pressing together and the pulling apart of things. Tension is at the core of its creativity. Nelson took us to the edge with that one note. He took us to that place of wonder, questioning, enjoyment—and *tension*.

We gave him a standing ovation.

Lord of the Paradox

Tension is conflict and contradiction, seeming contradiction, and living between what is and what should be. Tension is the origin of jazz; after all, jazz was produced by those who were "unfree in a free land."

Jazz became jazz in New Orleans. It was in "The Crescent City" that this tension became creative tension. In this diverse city of enslaved and free Africans, French, Swiss, and other Europeans, this remarkable form of existing came into being. New Orleans was a city of contradictions. For example, as a port city, it was instrumental for the North American slave trade, yet it simultaneously boasted the largest free population of former slaves in the South. In New Orleans, jazz took on the tension that existed in society.

It is about freedom within constraints. Play what

you want, but play the song. Just look at a jazz ensemble and the instruments they are playing. Some are pounded on; others require breath, while still others you pluck—sticks, brass, and strings. The drums have the ability to play loudly while the stand-up bass needs everyone to turn down the volume in order for it to be heard. Add to that the roles the musicians play and how these roles change from leading to supporting. The relationships between the players change the song. Are they mad at each other? Did they just have a disagreement over who gets paid what? Is the drummer not keeping the beat, or does the trumpet player always come in late or solo too long?

Not all tension is good, of course, and I'm not arguing for tension for tension's sake. But I do think that—because of the discomfort it brings—we try to remove it too quickly when it could be the very thing that would allow us to see things differently and go places we wouldn't have been able to go. Think about it. What makes it possible for cars to drive suspended over the waters of the San Francisco Bay on the Golden Gate Bridge? It's a "tension" bridge. New realities emerge because of competing pressures. In our faith this has the potential to take us places we otherwise would have missed.

Could it be that one of the major reasons we lack creativity is that we have sought to remove the tension

from our faith? Attending church with people of similar status, class, race, and generation may reduce certain tensions, but perhaps we've closed the door on
something beautiful at the same time. We must stop
and ask ourselves if it is a good thing when wholesale
movements of younger generations press on and seek
to move forward while leaving our elders behind. No
doubt it can be easier to exclude those who "can't keep
up" or meet the test of "survival of the fittest" because
they are deemed to not understand relevance. But the
path of least resistance may not be all that it's cracked
up to be, for it is in tension that we discover a more
creative way.

I pastor an interdenominational church. Not non-
denominational but interdenominational. The distinc-
tion is an important one. I know most churches that
use the "non" designation mean that they are not officially affiliated with a denomination. I much prefer
"inter" because it forces me to open my tradition of the
Christian faith to that of others. I grew up Southern
Baptist and then spent eight years in a Presbyterian
church. I am forever grateful for those experiences.
I am only enriched by the different views on church
structure and the sacraments (or observances, depending on your perspective). This doesn't mean I do not
have strong beliefs—surely I do. But I am addicted to
what happens when we are willing to coexist inter-

denominationally. I can't get enough of how much this community sharpens my own faith in Christ. Trust me—it can be very interesting when you have Catholics, Baptists, African-Methodist Episcopalians, and tongue-speaking Pentecostals all in community together!

The Lord of Paradox

I'm glad to have discovered James Lucas's insightful book *Knowing the Unknowable God,* in which he says that our God is "the Lord of Paradox." Not contradictions but paradox—impossible possibilities. Lucas contends that—contrary to popular belief—the Bible is full of these paradoxes. "Thumb through your Bible," he writes, "and you'll be overwhelmed by paradoxes. Resist your enemies *and* love them. Ignore hypocritical spiritual leaders *and* obey them. Forget what's in your past *and* be careful to remember. Flee from evil *and* stand firm against it. Don't judge *and* judge rightly."[11] Lucas argues that the goal is not to remove the mystery but to embrace it because—in the process—we will discover God in a different way. After all, it is God who is choosing to reveal himself in this way. I've stopped listening to sermons that purport to explain it all away, and I no longer read books that offer the Scriptures devoid of seeming contradiction. I'd rather take them for what they are—the words of the most creative being in the universe.

As one who has spent much time in my study of the Scriptures trying to resolve anything that seems contradictory, this has been refreshing. I used to see two passages that might disagree and then work hard to prove why they are just "seeming" or "apparent" contradictions. On the one hand, this approach gives us a Bible we can believe in; on the other hand, we must be careful not to remove the reasons to believe in the God it proclaims. It is fundamental to have a Scripture that can be defended and shown to be the word of God. However, there is also something to be gained by wrestling with it and with the God it presents.

Lucas describes an ancient way of interpreting the Bible, one that he argues Jesus used. It's called "halakic reasoning." Simply put, it's holding both strands of a paradox in tension and balance, knowing that with God both sides must be true. It's the process of firmly grabbing *both* ideas in paradox and then merging the two into a greater understanding of the character and nature of God. What the ancient Hebrews called "halakic," we call jazz!

This kind of thinking requires that we grip competing truths equally and see where they take us. We can do this, for while the Bible contains "no real contradictions," it does contain plenty of paradoxes. The goal, writes Lucas, is to "grab on to both sides" and see that they actually "complement, reinforce, and enhance each other."[12] Instead of resolving tension, we search for it. When discovered, we use it to enhance and deepen our relationship with our Creator.

Tertium Quid

The woman had been "caught in adultery."[13] The religious leaders bring her to Jesus in all of her shame, publicly exposing her sin as they fire their accusation: "Teacher, this woman was caught in the act of adultery. In the Law Moses commanded us to stone such women." (And men, I might add!)

"Now what do you say?" they ask Jesus, trying to trap him. They think they have him impaled on the horns of a dilemma, but Jesus knows what to do with tension.

He adds to the mystery of the moment by bending down and writing in the sand. He then embraces the paradox and turns the tension into creativity: "If any one of you is without sin, let him be the first to throw a stone at her."

These two opposing truths provided a whole new option for those present that day — a third way (in Latin, *tertium quid*), a new, creative way. This happens when we move beyond either/or to both/and. This is the gateway to improvisation. Jazz is the willingness to live between freedom and unfreedom and see where it leads. Jazz is the inclination to seek the interplay between life and death, right and left, up and down. When we embrace tension, we see multiple realities that are simultaneously true and lead us to the tertium quid thinking of Jesus.

This is not easy. When Jesus spoke to the accusing religious leaders here in John 8, there were some who felt that the word of God wasn't being fully obeyed and others who had to face the fact that they themselves had not lived up to the words of God. Can you imagine how the third-way thinking of Jesus would revolutionize Christianity today?

What if we were ...

liberal *and* conservative

Republicans *and* Democrats

critics *and* supporters

sinners *and* saints

full of grace *and* truth?

Jazz thrives on tension, and a jazz-shaped faith will discover the wonder of improvisation if we are willing to embrace opposing views at the same time. This leads to a new way of Christian thinking—a way where we are not arguing and debating all the time but pursuing and discovering the creative way, which will, hopefully, be the kingdom way.

> Nonviolent direct action seeks to create such a crisis and establish such creative tension that a community that has constantly refused to negotiate is forced to confront the issue. It seeks to dramatize the issue so that it can no longer be ignored.... I am not afraid of the word *tension.* I have earnestly worked and preached against violent tension, but there is a type of constructive nonviolent tension that is necessary for growth.
>
> **Martin Luther King Jr., in a letter from the Birmingham city jail**

When I speak of embracing paradox, I'm not trying to be wishy-washy about truth. I believe in absolute truth, and I believe that truth can be known. I just don't want to know it so well that it loses its intrigue. I think that is why I love the sound of a muted trumpet. There is something about muffled and tinny notes. You can hear them—but not fully. That is how I see the truth of God revealed to us. The mystery of the gospel is truth in disguise. Muted truth. It exists, but it is veiled enough to keep us searching. The gospel is a mystery revealed. But just because the mystery is now known doesn't mean it is any less mysterious. Ultimately, I think that God keeps truth mysterious because truth is not a concept; truth is a person—Jesus[14]—and he will forever be a mystery to unravel.

Return to Mystery, Return to Romance

How do you find a honeycomb in the woods? Henry
David Thoreau suggests that you must find some flow-
ers and wait for a bee to land. Then proceed to trap
the bee with a glass and piece of paper. Proceed to an
open area, release the bee, and chase it for as long as
you can. When you can no longer keep up with or see
the little critter, find another flower and wait. Keep
repeating the process until you see a bee fly into the
hive.[15]

God is mysterious, and his gospel is a mystery. Mysteries are meant to be pursued. As soon as they are
solved they cease to be mysteries. Maybe that's why
God is keeping secrets from us. Perhaps that's why he
hides things—important things. Solomon wrote, "It is
the glory of God to conceal a matter; to search out a
matter is the glory of kings."[16]

The gospel is a paradox in and of itself—a mystery
revealed *and* a mystery concealed. Paul speaks of this
revealed mystery in Colossians when he writes,

I have become [the church's] servant by the com-
mission God gave me to present to you the word
of God in its fullness—the mystery that has been
kept hidden for ages and generations, but is now
disclosed to the saints. To them God has chosen
to make known among the Gentiles the glorious

riches of this mystery, which is Christ in you, the hope of glory.[17]

Thanks be to God that the mystery has been revealed. The good news is Christ in us. However, this new information comes with more mystery. I remember when our oldest daughter first began to ask questions about Jesus. She wanted to know where Jesus was, and so we said, "He's in your heart." She responded, "Get him out of there!" When we talked to her about Jesus being her best friend, she was much more receptive. Her reaction was natural for a literal-minded four-year-old. But we adults shouldn't think that we understand it either. It's still a mystery.

Jesus spoke of the kingdom as a mystery. He said that God purposely hides that which is most vital to life. It isn't that it is lost; rather, it has been hidden by God himself. There is a reason Jesus calls us to *seek* the kingdom.

> Jesus said, "I praise you, Father, Lord of heaven and earth, because you have hidden these things from the wise and learned, and revealed them to little children."[18]

The kingdom is for those who like a child will run headlong into the field looking for buried treasure because her Father in heaven said it is there and worth finding.[19] The kind of person who would seek the kingdom is the kind of person who would chase a honeybee with the hope of finding the secret place. If we choose to seek this pearl of great price, we will find all that our soul desires—but we will also have to learn to live with the mystery and tension of a God who hides things from us. Hides himself from us? I think God wants to be searched for. I think he wants to be found.

Like any relationship of love, when we remove the mystery, we remove the romance. When we are curious about someone, we don't seek to explain away what we don't understand about them. No, we lean forward at the dinner table and ask questions. Too many times we take on the tone of a lawyer instead of one who is in love when we ask questions of God. There is a difference between asking God questions and questioning God. We wonder why the romance wanes. Freshness in any relationship has elements of expectation and mystery. They are the stuff of romance. If we are going to remember our "first love,"[20] we will need to guard the embers and stoke the flames of this love. This will require that we let God be God—mysterious and paradoxical though he is.

When we remove the tension, we remove the romance. When we remove the romance, we can quickly feel stuck in a rut. But don't worry—a rut is when you are caught between tension on both sides. You can look up and see a new perspective, a third perspective. When we are in a rut with God, we can stop and realize that a rut only exists because there are two opposing, competing, and equally strong forces that create sides. Those sides create a groove. Creative tension helps us to find the groove.

A Love Supreme

Let's talk some more 'Trane. John Coltrane eventually had to come to terms with the paradox of his life. He could play anything except the one thing he wanted to play most: the sound of God that he heard in 1957. After years of searching he embraced this tension and allowed it to fuel creativity. In 1964, seven years after he had heard the sound, he recorded his signature album, *A Love Supreme*. It is a case study in spiritual creativity. What do you do when you have experienced God and yearn to experience him again? Coltrane developed his own set of spiritual stages on this album, as each song is meant to represent a season of his soul. Coltrane's stations were *acknowledgment*, *resolution*, *pursuance*, and *psalm*.

Coltrane set a spiritual goal: to become a psalm. Working backward from that end, he thought through the stages necessary to achieve this goal. Ultimately, what was driving him is captured in the title of the album—*A Love Supreme*. That is all he wanted and all he wanted to be. What do you think of Coltrane's stations?

On the one hand, we could take them on as our own and seek to move through each stage ourselves. And that would be a noble goal. However, a jazz-shaped faith is not about merely copying other people's walk with God, but about recognizing that our relationship with God will be the most unique relationship that we have and that God has a special connection with each of his children. Surely we should learn from others who have drawn near to God, as long as it's about being inspired by them to create and discover the Spirit's song *for ourselves*. This is why many saints throughout the centuries have organized their lives around stages—very personal movements that corresponded with the work of the Holy Spirit's breathing in their life. Saint Teresa of Avila and Saint John of the Cross sought to understand the reoccurring stages that the Spirit was leading them through. Do you find yourself cycling through stages in your relationship with the Lord? Have you listened to them? Owned them? Sought a love supreme? Any Christian spirituality must begin with Christ—basking in his love for us and realizing that we can now love as he loves.[21]

To do what Coltrane did is to cooperate with the way in which God is growing you spiritually and then to commit to display it in everyday life — "faith expressing itself through love."[22] Everyday life for a musician is music, and so Coltrane captures his stages with an album. For you it will be different, depending on whether you are a work-at-home mom or a banker, a baseball player or a painter. The test as to whether or not it is God's work in our lives is to note how well our spirituality survives in the midst of the minute and mundane tasks of life. It must be able to be lived in the midst of diapers and dishpans, leg lifts and laptops, lovemaking and grocery shopping. When we embed our spirituality so deep into our lives that it can exist not only when we are doing "spiritual things" but in the midst of our vocations and avocations, then we have discovered a jazz-shaped spirituality.

Con-Tension

Take a moment to read what Coltrane wrote on the original liner notes to *A Love Supreme*:

Dear Listener:
        ALL PRAISE BE TO GOD TO WHOM ALL PRAISE IS DUE.
        Let us pursue Him in the righteous path. Yes it is

true; "seek and ye shall find." Only through Him can
we know the most wondrous bequeathal.

During the year 1957, I experienced, by the grace
of God, a spiritual awakening which was to lead me
to a richer, fuller, more productive life. At that time,
in gratitude, I humbly asked to be given the means
and privilege to make others happy through music.
I feel this has been granted through His grace. ALL
PRAISE TO GOD.

As time and events moved on, a period of
irresolution did prevail. I entered into a phase
which was contradictory to the pledge and away
from the esteemed path; but thankfully, now and
again through the unerring and merciful hand of
God, I do perceive and have been duly re-informed
of His OMNIPOTENCE, and of our need for and
dependence on Him. At this time I would like to tell
you that NO MATTER WHAT ... IT IS WITH
GOD. HE IS GRACIOUS AND MERCIFUL. HIS
WAY IS IN LOVE, THROUGH WHICH WE ALL
ARE. IT IS TRULY—A LOVE SUPREME—.

This album is a humble offering to Him. An
attempt to say "THANK YOU GOD" through
our work, even as we do in our hearts and with our
tongues. May He help and strengthen all men in every
good endeavor....

May we never forget that in the sunshine of our

lives, through the storm and after the rain—it is all with God—in all ways and forever.
ALL PRAISE TO GOD.

> *With love to all, I thank you*
> *John Coltrane*[23]

Now here's the kicker: Coltrane was not a Christian. Though he was raised in his grandfather's church and was familiar with the ways of Christ, he pursued God outside of Christianity. Coltrane had had a profound encounter with God that was catalytic to his becoming drug free, and that experience had an acute effect on the rest of his life. However, full transformation never occurred.

This could be a bone of conTENSION! ("How can a non-Christian be an example of living the gospel?" you may be asking.) The fact that he never claimed to follow Christ should challenge us even more. In contrast to 'Trane, how do we explain *our* lack of spiritual creativity? We personally know the most creative Being in the universe, and yet we all too often don't reflect that privilege. We turn the faith into a series of dos and don'ts instead of a path that leads to a love supreme.

Studying the tension in Coltrane's life makes me want to revisit how I walk with Christ and how I introduce others to the way of Christ. This is where the key notes of syncopation, improvisation, and call-and-response come into play.

Jazz-Shaped Evangelism

Syncopation

I believe that everyone has a God-given creative tension in his or her life. That is, there is paradox in your life and mine, and it might be the very thing that God wants to use to reveal himself. There is a reason we identify with Paul as he honestly speaks of the war within—the good we want to do but don't do, and the bad we find ourselves doing even though we don't want to.[24] We love Peter for the same reasons. We too have told Jesus that we will die for him, only to fail miserably within hours.[25] Every plumber has a leaky faucet, and every mechanic has a spark plug that needs to be changed. As we listen to the lives of the unbelievers whom God has placed in our life, we need to listen for the offbeats. Sometimes it's the beautiful woman who acts so ugly or the strong man who isn't strong enough to handle his anger. Once we see the seeming contradictions and impossible possibilities, then we hold on to them and ask Jesus to reveal to us—by his Spirit—the third way.

Remember how fraught with paradox Peter was? "I will lay down my life for you," he promises Jesus, and then he seeks to back up his words with actions as he unsheathes his sword in the garden.[26] Yet, within hours, he has proceeded to cowardly disown Jesus three times.

Fast-forward. After the resurrected Jesus serves breakfast to Peter, Jesus asks him, "Simon son of John, do you truly love me more than these?"[27] With that question Jesus recognizes Peter's contradictions and impossible possibilities. He is Peter (the rock)—though Jesus calls him Simon, for he seems to be slipping back to his old self.

"More than these?" Was Jesus pointing to the 153 fish, asking Peter if he wanted to be a fisherman instead of a fisher of men? Or perhaps Jesus was motioning to the other disciples sitting around the fire. After all, Peter tried to act as if he were more faithful than them when he said, "Even if all fall away on account of you, I never will."[28]

Three times Jesus asks Peter if he loves him—one for each of his disownings. And with that the contradictions of Simon Peter are evident and the third way is presented—Peter the fisherman can now become a shepherd!

Improvisation

It is here that we take the risk of composing in the moment. We allow our time in God's Word to connect with what he has been doing in a person's life, and perhaps, by God's grace, the salvific paradigm will become evident.

Who we are will determine what questions we ask. My friend and trumpeter extraordinaire Hugh Ragin decided to read through the Bible in multiple translations. He had one question: "What is the role of the trumpet in the plan of God?" He discovered various places where horns and trumpets accompany the works and worship of God. Imagine what he felt when he realized that the ultimate question is not "What is the role of the trumpet in the will of God?" but "Who is the trumpet of God?" He still smiles when he talks about how he read these words: "On the Lord's Day I was in the Spirit, and I heard behind me a loud voice like a trumpet."[29]

The voice of Jesus is "like a trumpet." When Hugh teaches music and practices his craft, he does so with new meaning and hope. He plays the instrument that sounds like the voice of our Savior.

Call-and-Response

Tell me about the first time you experienced the presence of God? What if that question was how we began a conversation with an unbeliever? I believe that Coltrane had an encounter with God. All too often we think it is our job to get people in a place where they can call on God, but what if God has already called them? Then our role in someone's life is to help them respond to the overtures of God. The Scriptures are rife with examples of this.

God is calling to everyone. Jesus told us that the work of the Holy Spirit is to convict the world of its sin.[30] God is already speaking to people before they even recognize him. Paul says that God is calling out to people in *and* through creation.[31]

The Magi of the Christmas story were doing something they were not supposed to be doing—practicing astrology, seeking guidance in the stars. So what does God do? Gracefully, God called to them in their sin and gave them an astronomical experience that led them to Jesus the Messiah.[32]

Cornelius had been interacting with God long before Peter arrived at his house to share the gospel with him. Take a closer look at the story.[33] God called to Cornelius and told him that his piety and generosity toward the poor have not gone unnoticed and that he wanted him to speak with Peter. This centurion in the Italian Regiment responded to God's call and sent for the apostle. When Peter entered Cornelius's life, Cornelius had already had a profound experience with God and his angel. Peter's job was to assist this man in his response to God.

What if our role is akin to that of Eli in Samuel's life? Young Samuel was sleeping when God called. The word of God had not yet come to him, so he was not familiar with the voice of God. Samuel mistook God's call for that of Eli the priest. Eli sent the boy back to bed, only to have God call him again. On the third call, Eli realized what was happening. He saw that his role was to assist Samuel in responding to God's call. He then told Samuel, "Go and lie down, and if [God] calls you, say, 'Speak, LORD, for your servant is listening.'"[34] God called. Eli guided Samuel in his response.

Too many times, we assume unbelievers have had no experience with God. Coltrane, as well as many biblical examples, show us that we should examine our preconceived notions about the preconversion activity of God in the lives of people. Instead of always trying to get them to have an encounter with God, maybe we should assume they have already had one!

Think of someone in your life who is not a follower of Christ. Call this person up and take him or her out for coffee. Instead of trying to convince him or her of the things of God, just ask, "When was the first time you felt the presence of God?" When I ask this question, I am utterly amazed at the responses I have received.

Jazz-Shaped Spirituality

We need basic spiritual disciplines such as participating regularly in corporate worship and Bible reading, practicing generosity, and engaging in a life connected to the poor. A cursory reading of the Scriptures and the rudiments of Christian belief show us that. In addition to incorporating traditional spiritual disciplines into our life with Christ, we can use these jazz essentials (syncopation, improvisation, and call-and-response) to discover new vistas and venues for meeting God. A tailor-made personal spirituality, so to speak.

If we are rooted in the historic faith, basic Christian doctrine, and community, then I think we are ready to experiment a little. Take the same jazz-shaped questions, and answer them for yourself.

- *Syncopation*: What is the unspoken tension in my life that could be a source of creative tension?
- *Improvisation*: What is the third way that is presenting itself?
- *Call-and-Response*: Is God calling me and waiting for my response?

In my life the questions and answers all lead to my children. I am the father of six, and God is constantly calling to me through them. As I seek to show them my love, it is not hard to make the connection to what God must go through as my heavenly Father.

However, I have had to face an uncomfortable tension that children introduce into my relationship with God. When I didn't have children, I could sit down anywhere and open my Bible and spend time with God. I could have spontaneous time with my Savior without much interruption. Oh, how my life has changed! Sometimes I go into the bathroom just to find a moment alone. The tension of my spiritual life is that my wonderful children are gifts from God *and* a monumental challenge to spending time with God. Therein lies the dilemma that I must embrace. I am the father of six children who all need my time *and* I need to spend time with my Father in heaven. What do I do?

This creative tension has led me to pray in a way I never would have prayed earlier in my life. It involves my children and their names. Like most parents, my wife and I sought to give our children meaningful names. So now, as I spend time with them seeking to be the father they need, I use their names to simultaneously represent the cry of my heart to God.

Our oldest child is Selah. That's the little word you see sprinkled throughout the book of Psalms. Some say it means "to pause and reflect." The Psalter was the book of worship for Israel—the hymnal, so to speak. When we named her, Barbara's and my prayerful hope was that Selah would always be found in the midst of worship. How do I spend time with God and Selah? When I look into her eyes she reminds me that any moment is a moment in which I can pause and seek my Savior and that worship is foundational to knowing God.

*Lord, receive every moment of my life
as a sacrifice of praise.*

Kia Regina was our first adopted child. Regina means "royal one" or "royalty." We so much want Kia to know that she is chosen. We chose her, and—even more important—God chose her to be in a family with Jesus, the King of kings. Our verse for her is 1 Peter 2:9, which speaks of God's people being "chosen," "royal," "holy," and "belonging."

*Lord, help me to live as a co-heir
with Christ.*

Gabriel—"God's hero." It's the name of the angel who announced the good news to so many people at the time of Jesus' birth. As I watch my oldest son turn regular clothes hangers into multiuse combination bow-and-arrow machine guns, I marvel at his innate courage and strength. I so much want him to see that God has given him power and muscles not to hurt people but to help people.

*Lord, I desire to do acts of love for the sake
of your kingdom. Make me strong enough
to live and love like Jesus.*

James is named after the brother of Jesus, whose nick-name was "Camel Knees" because he spent so much time kneeling in prayer that his knees were calloused like those of a camel. The book of James was also the first book of the Bible that I read when I was nine years old. I have forever been struck by the kind of faith that is portrayed in that book. There's plenty of prayer fodder there.

Lord, bring about justice in this world
for the poor and the orphan.
Jesus, teach me to pray, just as you taught
your disciples to pray.

Our fifth child, Mihret, is from Ethiopia, and her name means "mercy of God" in Amharic. I was born in 1969 at Mercy Hospital, and she is a reminder to me that "surely goodness and mercy shall follow me all the days of my life."[35] I join with all of those in Scripture who prayed the most prayed prayer in the Bible:

Kyrie eleison—Lord, have mercy!

Finally, there is Temesgen, who is Ethiopian as well. He was brought to the orphanage a few months after his birth. We don't know his exact birth date or what his life was like for those first formative months. We are comforted, though, because in the paperwork given us on the day he arrived, the man who brought him signed his name, *Immanuel.* How do you say thank you to God, who has been too good to you? In Amharic there is a word reserved for those moments of overwhelming gratitude for all of our cups that overflow — Temesgen means "thanks be to God." My son's name is my prayer.

Temesgen! Temesgen! Temesgen!
For all of your goodness in my life and
for always being Immanuel, God with us.

The process of playing and praying has gone a long way toward helping me live a life of unceasing prayer, and it gives my children the attention they deserve. For with each name I have a new prayer.

How long will I pray in this manner? For as long as it allows me to be a man of prayer and a man who pays attention to his children. What would it look like for you to be more creative in your relationship with God? Wouldn't you love to find out?

CHAPTER 5

LIFE IN CONCERT

What if we experienced church like a jazz ensemble (listening to the beat of the image of God in each of us), and what if community meant that you and I felt connected, not only to those that we can see, but also with those who have followed (in past generations) and have yet (in future generations) to follow Jesus?

We were all created for community—
"beloved community."[1]

I write my sermons in coffee shops because I like being out of the office and in the presence of people who are going about their everyday lives. There is one coffee shop I've been going to for almost twenty years, and I vividly remember the first time I visited it. Above the cream and sugar there was a small handwritten sign that read: *European Style Seating, Join Someone at Their Table.*

That sign made me feel something. It awakened a desire—to connect and belong. It was then that I decided this was a place I wanted to be.

But here's the ironic thing: I have never joined anyone at his or her table. Nor do I want someone to actually pull up a chair and invade my sacred space. And therein lies the paradox of community. We desire freedom and the individuality that accompanies it, while at the same time we need to connect with others in the hope that someone will pull up a chair. We desire independence, but we don't want to be alone.

King's Nightmare

Most people know of the dream of Martin Luther King Jr., but few know of his nightmare. In 1963, King stood in the shadow of the statue of the man who authored the Emancipation Proclamation and called the nation "to live out the true meaning of its creed." With wondrous words and compelling cadence, he delivered one of the greatest sermons of all time. He called Americans to be American and Christians to be Christian. Few remained uninspired by a vision for what life could and should be.

Yet only four years later, Martin Luther King Jr. spoke of the same dream in very different and disturbing terms. On Christmas Eve 1967, before his home congregation, he said, "Not long after talking about that dream I started seeing it turn into a nightmare."[2]

What happened? What caused the man who had spoken such words of freedom and hope to pronounce such words of pessimism and gloom? Why did he lose heart in what had seemed so right?

Martin Luther King Jr.'s ultimate goal was grander than securing voting rights and achieving desegregation. He defined his mission as "genuine intergroup and interpersonal living."[3] As a Baptist preacher he believed that the way you change society is by changing the human heart, but there was a crisis in America that didn't allow for that option. On a daily basis, people were legally dehumanized through a system of laws known as "Jim Crow." In the South, separate bathrooms and schools were the norm, and lynchings were a common experience. As Billie Holiday sang, there was "strange fruit" hanging from Southern trees. Life was different but not much better in the North. Lack of jobs and opportunity led to increasing nihilism and despair. Something had to be done to put an end to the horrors and sorrow.

When King spoke of the dream, he didn't want to just stop what was wrong with America; he wanted that which was right. The dream was a summons for the church to be fertile soil for the kingdom of God and to nourish a unique expression of God's reign known as *the beloved community*—this was and is *the dream behind the dream* of Martin Luther King Jr.

To Martin Luther King Jr., the dream was the beloved community and the beloved community was the dream. True integration is what he envisioned. He communicated this on many occasions. In speeches and writing he said ...

> The end is reconciliation; the end is redemption; the end is the creation of the beloved community.

> The aftermath of nonviolence is the creation of the beloved community. The aftermath of nonviolence is redemption. The aftermath of nonviolence is reconciliation. The aftermath of violence is emptiness and bitterness.

> Our ultimate goal is integration, which is genuine intergroup and interpersonal living. Only through nonviolence can this goal be attained, for the aftermath of nonviolence is reconciliation and the creation of the beloved community.[4]

The originators of jazz were a second generation out of slavery and victims of rigorous forms of segregation in which humanity was routinely and institutionally denied. You would think that they were thinking about getting revenge, but in

> actuality, they were thinking about sharing and communicating with all kinds of people, and they became masters of achieving balance with others. These early jazz musicians worked out a perfect way to co-create using improvisation and a basic unity of rhythm called swing.
>
> **Wynton Marsalis, jazz musician**

Martin Luther King Jr. believed that it was possible for community to be experienced even with those who sought to cause you harm. That's why he chose the tactic of nonviolence to spark the creation of the beloved community. Nonviolence is the weapon of love. This method seeks to expose evil without harming the person perpetrating the evil. Its goal is to meet physical force with soul force. So if there was a person stinging your skin with water forced through a fire hose when all you wanted was the right to vote, or if dogs were released to attack when all you wanted was to use the same restroom as everyone else, retaliation was not an option. Nonviolence draws on the teaching of Jesus: "I tell you, Do not resist an evil person. If someone strikes you on the right cheek, turn to him the other also."[5]

The goal is to expose evil and then apply the remedy, all without causing harm. If you strike back at an enemy, he or she will most likely remain your enemy when the conflict has passed. But if you respond with love, then it is possible to extend the hand of friendship to the one who has harmed you—in search of common ground, higher ground.

Drastic times called for drastic means, so King focused his energy on changing laws through nonviolence in the hope that Christians would then focus on the real challenge of transforming hearts to catch up with the laws. And therein lies the problem, the reason the dream turned into a nightmare. The church wasn't up to the task. We had not fully understood the gospel and the community that it creates. We had not knelt with blood-sweating Jesus the night before he hung on the cross and agreed with him as he prayed:

> "My prayer is not for them alone. I pray also for those who will believe in me through their message, *that all of them may be one*, Father, just as you are in me and I am in you. May they also be in us so that the world may believe that you have sent me. I have given them the glory that you gave me, *that they may be one as we are one*: I in them and you in me. May they be brought to *complete unity* to let the world know that you sent me and have loved them even as you have loved me."[6]

Changed laws could only restrict behavior, but transformed hearts could create new behaviors. Yet for some reason the church continued to live according to the same patterns of society. As many have pointed out, racially speaking, the church went from separate pews to separate buildings. Or as sociology professor Michael Emerson poignantly puts it, "Desegregation can be legislated. Integration, the ultimate goal, cannot.... Desegregation creates the condition 'where elbows are together and hearts apart.' "[7]

King's nightmare was personal. When you read his "Letter from Birmingham Jail," you can feel his lament as he pleads with fellow clergy to see what seemed so obvious to him in the Scriptures. He wrote from behind bars, calling church leaders to see the "interrelatedness of all communities and states." He called them to a holy, sacramental endeavor of collecting facts to determine injustices, negotiation, self-purification, and direct action on behalf of the body of Christ. He wrote,

> In deep disappointment, I have wept over the laxity of the church. But be assured that my tears have been tears of love. There can be no deep disappointment where there is not deep love. Yes, I love the church; I love her sacred walls. How could I do otherwise?... Yes, I see the church as the body of Christ. But, oh! How we have blemished and scarred that body through social neglect and fear of being nonconformists.[8]

Most instruments used in jazz do not sound good by themselves. It is only when they are blended with others that they become compelling. To choose to be a jazz musician is to choose to live in community. So it is with responding to the call of Christ. The gospel is about the individual *and* the group. When we make a "personal" decision to follow Jesus, it is simultaneously a decision to join a community. The moment we ask Jesus into our hearts, we become part of his people as well. Salvation isn't just an individual experience; it's communal as well. To follow Jesus is to become part of God's chosen people, the body of Christ. The Scriptures tell us that we are chosen by God and adopted as his children.[9] However, we are not an only child; our adoption makes us part of an extremely diverse family that has a "firstborn" son with whom we are co-heirs.[10] Responding to the call of the gospel is to respond as an "I" *and* a "we."

We make individual decisions to be a Christian, but it is impossible to follow Jesus by ourselves. As soon as we begin our journey with Jesus, we hear him say things like,

> "A new command I give you: Love one another. As I have loved you, so you must love one another. By this all men will know that you are my disciples, if you love one another."[11]

"Love your neighbor as yourself."[12]

Hearing words like these makes us realize that following Jesus is intricately connected with others. It's a beautiful challenge to be part of Christ's community, realizing that in the garden of Eden there was perfect relationship with God and each other and that as God restores a right relationship with him, he also restores us to those around us. Jesus' death on the cross broke down every barrier that could keep us from God *and* from each other.[13] So much so that when the apostle John gets a glimpse of heaven, he points out that there are people there from every tribe, language, people, and nation.[14] In heaven our differences don't disappear. Have you ever thought about that? What color will you be in heaven? Your skin will be the same beautiful color it is now.

When we gather together in our local church, we have the opportunity to give witness to the reconciling work of Christ as we worship and serve in unity across racial, denominational, cultural, and economic divides. What's fun about this is that God leaves us to display this unity in our own way. Each culture gets to dig within itself to discover how the "I" and the "we" are lived out practically. What this means is this: *While the good news of Christ is transcendent, there are a myriad of ways to actualize it in community.* How we do this depends on each culture's definition of community. We need to put on our "missionary eyes" and look at how our own culture defines community because too much is at stake to fall asleep at the wheel!

The Greatest Partnership That Never Happened

We were created for community, and as a community we point to the love of God. This is why I lamented when I first encountered the story of the never fully formed alliance between Martin Luther King Jr. and Billy Graham.[15] Wouldn't it have been great if these two icons had joined forces? What a team they would have been—black and white, standing for spiritual and social transformation! They thought about it. In 1957, Billy Graham invited King to pray at a crusade he was holding in New York City. King and Graham strategized about holding joint crusades that would be open to all people. They became close enough that Graham called King by his nickname, Mike. But there were too many unresolved issues, and it has been called "the greatest partnership

> In jazz, it is the activity itself that is as important as the result. It is a music that is learned in the doing, in collective play: it is a social music.
>
> John F. Szwed, anthropologist and jazz expert

that never happened." I wish they had allowed jazz to shape their faith. This alternative way was developing right alongside them and would have shown them what to do with the tensions they were facing. What's more, jazz would have provided a unique option to their relationship.

E Pluribus Unum

E pluribus unum—out of many, one. This motto represents the American desire to be a society in which people from the whole world can come and participate. At first, it only referred to the original thirteen colonies, but over time we have come to recognize that the United States is a nation created from the nations. Community in America begins with understanding that we are many—native and immigrant, French, Italian, German, Spanish, and so on—and while the story of how we came to be on these shores is different, we can be one. *E pluribus unum* appears on the Great Seal of the United States and on much of our money, and it represents our quest and question when it comes to community in our culture.

It's a laudable goal, but how do you make many into one? The answer depends on your metaphor. The image we have in our mind for community is vital, not just for our country, but for church as well, for our culture will guide our pursuit toward being one in Christ.

The melting pot was (and still is for many) a guiding metaphor for making one out of many. It is the idea that when a potential new citizen arrives, he or she assimilates into a common culture that brings about unity. The hope is that whatever we let go of will more than be returned in the land of opportunity. Many gladly melt into this "great crucible" for the benefits it affords. Others wonder if the cost is too high as they simmer in the stew and give way to a new culture. Some who find the melting process difficult can't quite liquefy and become the sludge at the bottom of the pot. Ultimately, the melting pot is more about the one than the many—which is why many opt for the salad bowl as a more fitting metaphor.

In a salad, lettuce remains lettuce and tomatoes remain tomatoes. The salad bowl seeks to move beyond the melting pot by drawing attention to the need for individuality. The salad dressing becomes the key—representing that which keeps everything together. But what is the dressing? What is that one common thing that holds us all together? Some have said it is democracy, which is a pretty good answer for a country but a bad answer for a church. How united in Christ can we be if everything comes down to votes? I win, you lose—

and vice versa. A good attempt, but it's more about the many than the one.

We must be careful not to fall into the pitfalls of either of these metaphors while at the same time recognizing that *e pluribus unum* is compatible with the gospel's call to community. While both metaphors have strengths, the cost of their weakness is too high. We desperately need a new way of thinking about community in America. A fresh paradigm that will help bring about unity among churches and within local bodies of believers. A way of being "I" and "we"—so we don't reduce our definition of community to "being in a small group." What is community? Is it having significant relationships with others? Is it the people who live in your same geographic space? I believe it's all that and so much more.

Becoming Pentecostal

At Babel, one became many. At Pentecost, many became one.

How do you make one out of many? That has been the question for the church since the first century. I remember hearing British author and former pastor Roy Clements say that all human forms of unity usually try to make people one by making them the same. Communism tried this through imposed ideology, and the military does so through uniforms and a common code. Ultimately it is the Spirit of God who shows us the way of unity without uniformity.

We see this so clearly in Acts 2 when the Holy Spirit brought together a crowd that was as diverse as any city we live in today. The miracle of tongues was that each person heard the apostles speaking in his or her own language. Here they are—allowed to receive the gospel and affirm that there is "one Lord, one faith, one baptism,"[16] while at the same time to remain who they were.

No metaphor can adequately address everything. Ultimately, it is the Holy Spirit who brings about the unity that is needed to represent people of the gospel. That being said, I believe we have a better metaphor for the Spirit to use—one that will allow each of us to play one song with our many instruments for the glory of God.

Because it is unique to America, jazz also has struggled with *e pluribus unum* and offers an alternative to the imagery of the melting pot and the salad bowl. It points us in a fresh direction. Think about it. What is it that allows the same people to play the same song night after night and yet still be interested in each other and what they are doing? What allows a jazz musician from one city to walk into a venue in another city and join a group she has never played with—and yet they sound as if they have jammed together on many an occasion?

The answer in one word: *ensemble*.

Ensemble Community

I suggest that ensemble can be the alternative metaphor to the melting pot and the salad bowl.

The *American Heritage Dictionary* defines ensemble as "a unit of complementary parts that contribute to a single effect" (from Old French, *together*, and Late Latin, *at the same time*). Ensemble community balances the individual and the group. Watch any jazz ensemble, and it is difficult to listen to the whole without also listening to the parts. When a song is in full swing, you can appreciate the collective sound, you can focus in on the bass player as he runs a scale in time with the drummer, or you can give your attention to the pianist, who could carry the whole tune by herself and yet is playing for and with the other members of the group. At once, they operate as individuals and a unit. Bound by the song but not constrained by it. One and yet many.

> Jazz is freedom music,... the one-and-many *e pluribus unum* with a laid-back beat.
> **Robert G. O'Meally, jazz expert**

Observe a jazz ensemble. Let your mind wander.

What would it be like to do community in this way? What are the implications of thinking of each instrument as individuals—in your Bible study, with fellow colleagues on a church staff, or as individual churches in a city? After all, when Jesus looks at the church in a city, he only sees one church. Remember the seven churches that Jesus addresses in Revelation 2–3? He speaks to the church in Laodicea, Ephesus, Smyrna, and so on. These are the names of the cities in which the church was meeting and serving. It is safe to assume they were not all meeting in one place, just as the church in Denver, Los Angeles, and Chicago meets in hundreds of locations. Though the churches are many, Jesus referred to them as one.

Ensemble is a homegrown metaphor. It is a product of our own culture's desire and struggle for *e pluribus unum*. As such, it is an alternative paradigm for Christian community that can help us face the challenges of race, denomination, and class that so divide the body of Christ. Core to jazz is the existence of the individual within a group in which both the unity of the group and the freedom of the individual are valued. "Solo-darity," if you will.

Life in Concert: More Than Meets the Ear*

Not too long ago, I went to a performance of one of my favorite jazz ensembles. They had been doing a lot of rehearsing and had finally found their groove. Some background music played as they took the stage for their second set. As the music faded, the trumpeter looked at the speaker, picked up on the last note, and continued the song that was playing. For the next minute or two, the others followed along, and then they seamlessly transitioned into an original composition I had heard them do on previous occasions. And then came the biggest surprise.

As the pianist neared the end of his solo, he realized that he was not only playing with his present ensemble, but the late John Coltrane was on stage too! Somehow the pianist had begun to play Coltrane's classic "A Love Supreme." As he began the unmistakable groove, the rest of the band followed, and they played a few more minutes on that note.

Jazz ensembles are communities of the past, present, and future. When a musician takes the stage they do so in recognition of those who have played the songs before them. Jazz is about tradition as well as respect

---

* A phrase borrowed from Paul F. Berliner, author of *Thinking in Jazz: The Infinite Art of Improvisation* (Chicago: Univ. of Chicago Press, 1994).

for the founders and innovators. That is why on jazz radio stations the DJ will tell you who composed the song and who was playing what instrument. It's about the many and the one; that includes the many who have preceded. The same is true with Christianity.

I've concluded that I need to enlarge my view of community. It is normal to consider community only in terms of the present; that is, who are the people whom I know, worship with, and pray with now. If we get radical, we also realize that community is not just about who we know and have a relationship with, but that it includes all Christians who are alive at the same time we are. This being true, we find ourselves praying for Christians in other countries who are facing difficulties and persecution. As I read the Bible, community is all of this and so much more. Christians are called to live in community not only with those in the present but also with those in the past and the future.

> Jazz is one long chain [and] will still be played ... as long as its sources are remembered.
> **Studs Terkel, author and historian**

When God would introduce himself in the Old Testament, he would sometimes say, "I am the God of Abraham, Isaac and Jacob."[17] That is, as he was doing something in someone's life in the now that would affect future generations, it was important to him that the continuity and connection with what he had done with saints gone by be maintained. With that multi-generational introduction, God helps us see that to know *him* is to know *them* as well. We are to live today in light of those who lived yesterday. Hebrews 12 reminds us of the "great cloud

> He must learn the best of the past, and add to it his personal vision.
>
> **Ralph Ellison, author and jazz expert**

of witnesses" who cheer us on as we run the same race they did. In the early centuries of the church, when someone died, his or her picture would be placed on the wall in the place of worship, for the person had not died; rather, he or she had simply joined the heavenly worship service. As believers worshiped on earth, they did so with the understanding that those from their past are also part of their future. They viewed themselves as *actively* in communion with those who had faithfully followed Christ, and as living for the day when they would join them. In light of this, our modern-day view of community seems so myopic, self-centered, and shortsighted.

Life in Concert: More Than Meets the Eye

Improvisation is not random or accidental; rather, it is a social experiment. When a soloist steps into the break that the band has provided and begins to improvise, it doesn't mean he is making things up on the spot without any forethought. All too often we think that improvisation is an off-the-cuff, in-the-moment performance; however, if you talk to those who actually do it, you hear a different story. Improvisers are still composing, but they are composing in the moment, and that moment is the result of many variables. Among them are the assumptions and expectations that the members have of each other based on the previous time they've spent together.

I have a friend who is involved in improv theatre. He and his comedy team walk on stage, take random suggestions from the audience, and then proceed to make up a lengthy skit on the spot. It looks off-the-cuff and magical, but I know he and his team work hard making things up in the moment. He attends workshops and seminars and spends hours in rehearsal. In addition to practicing various scenarios so they become familiar with each other's cues, they continually evaluate each other.

The same is true in a jazz ensemble. Even if you have never played in a band, you can observe that an ensemble is operating with a set of agreements, assumptions, and expectations that allow for freedom within community. Doing so allows them to take turns, moving in and out of supporting roles and lead roles without conversation. Jazz music is a group experience in which the members work on the fluency of their shared language of spontaneity.

Improvisation is far from a random endeavor. As a matter of fact, before an ensemble even takes the stage, there are agreements that have already been made. These assumptions make improvisation possible without chaos. The number one agreement is the song. For this very reason I think a jazz-shaped faith is more than possible—because we have the Song of all Songs—Jesus—"the Word [that] became flesh."[18] Jesus lived among us, set the groove, and called out a melody of love, redemption, and freedom.

Ensemble Community: Practice Assumed

In ensemble community it is assumed that you know your instrument, have memorized the basic songs (called standards), and have practiced. Can you imagine how these three assumptions could change what you expected of others and what was expected of you at church? Wouldn't it be nice if you could assume that fellow Christians were proficient and experienced when it comes to the essentials of the faith? Wouldn't it be nice if other believers could assume that we know not only basic doctrine but live it as well? Shouldn't other Christians be able to assume that I love my enemies and turn the other cheek? Mastery is not necessarily expected, nor is flawlessness, but a basic understanding of the essential grooves and riffs is not only needed but expected.

When you meet a person who is Jewish, the natural question that comes to mind is, "Cultural or practicing?" By this we mean, does this person claim the title based on birth and heritage or based on actual lifestyle. I think we're at that place when it comes to Christianity. The term *Christian* is so widely used in America that it has almost become something many people claim by virtue of birth. As a pastor, I can't tell you the number of times I've spoken with someone who claimed to be a Christian, yet they had no comprehension of the cross of Christ and what embracing the cross makes possible for us in this life and the life to come. Honestly, most people I've the privilege to lead to Christ would never say they were being converted; rather, they would say they were recommitting themselves to Christianity. Because of people's ease in claiming to be Christian, I think we may be at the place where the pertinent question is, "Are you a cultural Christian or a practicing Christian?"

Practicing Christianity

If I told you you were going with me tonight to hear someone who has practiced the trumpet for thirty years, what would you expect? Your hopes would be high, and you would anticipate hearing someone whose skills were highly developed. Perfection wouldn't be the standard, but surely it would be reasonable to look forward to an enjoyable performance. What if I told you I have practiced following Jesus for thirty years? What should you expect of me?

Wouldn't it be nice to be able to assume of any Christian whom you encounter that they are "practicing"—that they have a basic understanding of the essential groove of God and that, while perfection isn't expected, you can at least jam together? What would you like to be able to assume of everyone who calls themselves a Christian? What would your top three Christian practices be?

Are you a practicing Christian? This isn't meant to be a question of eternal salvation; instead, it's a community question: What are the things we can count on each other for?

Take Stephen, for example. The early church had a problem. A group of widows were being neglected when it came to daily provisions. The leaders decided that in order to minister to these widows, they needed a group of practicing Christians. Look at the qualifications they expected: "Brothers, choose seven men from among you who are known to be full of the Spirit and wisdom. We will turn this responsibility over to them."[19]

Now remember, these were the expectations for those who were going to "wait on tables." Stephen, "a man full of God's grace and power,"[20] was among this group, this ensemble. One day, he was arrested and did something truly remarkable. As an angry mob followed, he was dragged before the court, where he faced false charges. He was given a chance to explain himself. Read Acts 7, and see how Stephen proceeded to give everyone a history lesson about God's redemptive work on the earth through the centuries — *all from memory*! Most people would find this difficult to do even under calm circumstances; Stephen did it in the face of the pressure of knowing he was on the verge of being executed for his faith. That is a practiced, a proficient, Christian. (Have you ever noticed that Jesus gave him a standing ovation?)[21]

Mary, the mother of Jesus, is another great example. After she received the news from the angel that she was going to give birth to the Messiah, she immediately interpreted it in light of her community — past, present, and future. She did so in true jazz form, as she sang a song known as the Magnificat.

Take a few minutes to read Mary's Song in Luke 1:46–55, and then compare it to Hannah's Song in 1 Samuel 2. What becomes obvious is that Mary is improvising. She searched her memory for another woman who had been in a similar situation. Hannah was the closest she could come. Drawing on the past, she added her own voice to an ancient song and poured out her heart.

She had obviously been practicing! I've often wondered if I could do this. Could I receive news from an angel that God was going to totally disrupt my life and then draw on the right Scripture passage while seeing it in light of my current circumstances? Not bad for a teenage girl!

Church: A Safe Place to Practice

Church, in large part, is a rehearsal studio. When we gather in groups big and small, we are preparing and practicing for eternity. We know that in heaven we are going to worship before the throne of God, so we gather in worship for our weekly dress rehearsal for eternity. Jesus told us that if we are faithful with little, then he will give us the opportunity to be faithful with much when his kingdom comes in fullness.[22] In anticipation of living with Jesus and his angels in the life to come, we practice serving together in our local communities today. A jazz-shaped approach builds on this concept.

In jazz you not only *perform* in community; you *practice* in community too. Ensemble is a learning environment that allows the practiced and the practicing to interact and grow together. As ethnomusicologist Paul Berliner reminds us, the jazz community is a large, informal "educational system" that instills the basics and allows for experimentation—but beyond formal institutional training and necessary musical lessons, there are a number of informal experiences that fall under the category of "hangin' out and jammin'," to use Berliner's term.[23]

Casual Apprenticeships

Drummers hang out with drummers and horn players with horn players, learning from one another, enjoying a fraternity of common blessing. Church can and should be a safe place where we can develop the spiritual gifts we have in company with others who share the same gifting. This allows for peer-to-peer exchange, with veterans and novices sharing together. This need not be a formal program in your church; rather, it is the result of our realizing that we need each other. When we see someone with a similar giftedness, we engage him or her in dialogue. Over a cup of coffee we compare notes on the joys and struggles, as well as the nuts and bolts, of the calling that God has on our life. This seems to be what Samuel was doing with his school of the prophets.[24]

I dream of doing this someday. I would love to be

the resident jazz theologian at a college or seminary where I could create ensembles of pastors and students called to be pastors, preachers and those desiring to preach, community organizers

> The musician is always engaged in a dialogue or a conversation or even argument—not only, as in a jam session, with his peers, but also with all other music and musicians in the world at large. Indeed, his is an ongoing dialogue with the form itself.
>
> **Robert O'Meally, author and jazz expert**

and young activists in the making. The real fun happens when you begin to mix up the ensembles into jam sessions.

Jam Sessions

Not only is it good to hang out with those who are practicing the same instrument you play; there is also a need to practice with others who will play the same song but on a different instrument. Jam sessions are times when those with varying degrees of ability can come together and work out and work on some things. It is experience through practicing performance. Paul Berliner writes,

> As essential to students as technical information and counsel is the understanding of jazz acquired

directly through performance. In part, they gain experience by participating in one of the most venerable of the community's institutions, the jam session. At these informal musical get-togethers, improvisers are free of the constraints that commercial engagements place upon repertory, length of performance, and the freedom to take artistic risks.[25]

There are so many stories about the jazz pioneers who would play their paid gig until well past midnight, only to gather together and do some jammin' with each other.

The German pastor Dietrich Bonhoeffer died at the age of thirty-nine in a Nazi prison camp. He was hanged a few days before the Allies liberated Flossenburg. I'll never forget the first time I read his classic book on Christian community called *Life Together*— containing Bonhoeffer's insights into how and why community is so important and, more specifically, into what makes Christian community Christian? In the early 1930s, Bonhoeffer studied at a seminary in New York City and was a visiting pastor at a church in Harlem during the Jazz Age. While he never mentions jazz specifically (as far as I'm aware), I wonder what effect the ensemble ethos that he observed and experienced had on his thinking, albeit subconsciously. In any case, the kind of community that can be described as "life together" is not easy. It takes practice *together* but also when we are *alone*.

Time in the Woodshed

Ask any accomplished musician how they became proficient, and they will point to long, lonely hours of repetition—time spent playing scales, learning chords, and training fingers to move from one progression to another. Any skill requires that we spend the necessary time working on the fundamentals.

Jesus called his disciples together to learn his ways before they were expected to live life in concert for the entire world to see. And he also modeled the woodshed for them.

At daybreak Jesus went out to a solitary place.[26]

Jesus often withdrew to lonely places and prayed.[27]

Jesus went out to a mountainside to pray, and spent the night praying to God.[28]

The woodshed can't be forced on someone; it has to be desired. I have a friend who tells of time spent in lonely practice, not because he enjoys it, but because he enjoys what it allows him to do on stage. Jesus didn't force on his disciples time in the woodshed. He modeled it, waiting for them to finally ask for it: "One day Jesus was praying in a certain place. When he finished, one of his disciples said to him, 'Lord, teach us to pray.' "[29]

Do you struggle with your prayer life? Have you asked Jesus to teach you?

Ensemble community allows for the many to become one. It also requires practice. In jazz, if someone is not ready, they let them know. Consider what tenor saxophonist and clarinetist Lester Young (aka "Prez") once told a drummer who wasn't cutting it on stage. Between sets, the unpracticed musician had tried to make small talk. "Say, Prez, when was the last time we worked together?"

"Tonight," replied Lester.[30]

God — The Original Jazz Ensemble

What makes church safe is that it takes its cue from God. Jesus alluded to this when he prayed that we would live in unity. He asked "that all of them may be one, Father, just as you are in me and I am in you."[31] The triune God is our model for life together. God is the original jazz ensemble — complete with an eternal jam session that all of us are invited to join. Abraham, Isaac, Jacob, Sarah, Hannah, and Esther joined in long ago. Now it's our turn.

Life in concert with God — ultimately that is what we are practicing for.

At Colorado Community Church we have traditional worship spaces with pews that all face the same direction. But we also have what we call The Upper Room—a worship space designed to point to the kind of community we desire to be. When you walk in, you are welcomed by candlelit tables. As you take your seat, you realize something: you are facing toward others. The hope is that in this room the participants might experience what the disciples did in the original upper room. Food. Drink. Conversation with God and each other. Ensemble.

On one of the walls is a picture—Rublev's "Holy Trinity" icon—created by a fifteenth-century monk. In the background of this painting there are images based on the obscure story in Genesis 18 of Abraham and the three visitors at Mamre. You can faintly see a hill, tree, and house. Some say the hill represents the journey and trials of life, the tree symbolizes the life that comes from the death and sacrifice of the journey, and the house stands for the house of the father who is waiting for prodigals to return. In the foreground is a table.

Drawing on the revelation of God, Rublev undertook to capture the mystery of the Trinity. This icon has forever changed my relationship with God. It has helped me to pray, as well as to better understand what it means to know God. At the table all three persons of the Godhead sit. God the Father, on the left, lifts his hand, blessing the Son. God the Son, sitting in the center, has two fingers pointing toward the Spirit. The Father sends the Son, the Son sends the Holy Spirit. All one—distinct yet equal. All soloists in their own right and yet sharing the stage of history. God—the original jazz ensemble.

Forever they have sat in perfect communion and conversation around this table. Sometime in eternity past a triune desire came into being—a desire to fill the empty seats around the table. The second member of the Godhead rose from his seat only to return with a chalice of his own blood and placed it in the center of the table. The invitation is to all to come and become part of the conversation—the song—and to join the ensemble where there are many from every tribe, language, people, and nation.

Yet we are one.

finding your voice

What if there is another way to know the Scriptures? What if we experienced the word of God as a song that sets us free to compose, a melody that has room for our voices to join in with the ancients?

I was reading on a bench at Denver's open-air 16th Street Mall when I heard it—the song of a saxophone. I followed the sound to a man half a block away who was playing for tips. As I listened, I realized I had company. An Asian man stood to my right, and a homeless man sat rolling a cigarette, about ten feet to my left.

We then decided to make our contribution to the performance. My newfound homeless friend shouted, "Herbie Hancock!" And much to our pleasure, the musician obliged. We smiled at each other as we marveled at his skills. I shouted, "Coltrane's 'Alabama.'" Once again, he treated us to the song of our choice. There we were—black, white, Asian, and homeless—equally transfixed by the music. It was a joy.

It was quitting time, so the passersby were many and the saxophonist's instrument case was collecting tips as people tossed in change, mostly out of charity. Then I noticed the obvious: *This guy didn't need the money; he needed an audience.*

He was dressed in Gap-esque attire and most likely was a student at a local university. He wasn't just practicing; he was trying to find his voice. He could have stayed at home—alone in the woodshed—to work on his skills, but what he needed was the risk of community. What he needed were other people to help him become what he knew he was. He needed to play the songs of others until he could play them in a unique way—in his own way.

I was happy to perform my role.

A jazz-shaped Christianity is about how we grow and develop, how we "become," within the confines and in the presence of others. As we practice the ancient ways, we do so in the presence of others and with their input spurring us on until we discover or happen upon our own voice. Composing a jazz-shaped faith will take ensemble to the point that we discover *and* simultaneously contribute to others' finding their own voices. This concept of finding one's voice can be especially helpful when it comes to how we read and communicate the story of God's redeeming grace (recorded in our Bibles) and how we live it out (expressed in our calling)—the word without and the word within.

> The group lends its support as each member learns to discover her or his own voice.
>
> **Ann Pederson, professor of religion**

Like the young saxophonist on the street, we need to know the song. That is, we need to know the ways of Christ and then bring who we are into the mix. That's what I mean by finding your voice—bringing who you are to the song. This requires a deep and abiding love for the Scriptures. They are the external word of God. We can hold them. See them. Touch them. Study them. The Scriptures give us life when they connect to the word within, God's mysterious and mystical internal word known as *calling*. This calling must always be measured by the Scriptures, and when they line up—when our internal calling finds the melody of the eternal word of God—the groove moves those around us closer to God.

Scripture: The Eternal Melody

What are we supposed to do with our Bibles? They contain the very words of God handed down to us through human personality. Sixty-six books that all point to a Creator who is actively involved with his creation, seeking, wooing, and redeeming. So what are we supposed to do with them? The most obvious answer is that we are to read and study them. This, for me, still begs the questions: But how are we supposed to understand them? Interpret them? Live them? We spend much time studying the Scriptures alone and in groups. We sit and listen to preachers pontificate about the original settings and languages. We take notes. To what end?

Hermeneutics is the art and science of biblical interpretation. This approach to reading our Bibles uses the empirical method (make observations, collect data, come to a conclusion). The basic idea is that we can understand the meaning of the Scriptures primarily through cognitive measures. That is, we can "know" the Scriptures if we know how to study them or sit under the teaching of someone who knows.

In classical mythology, Hermes was the Greek god of secret knowledge. With wings on his head and feet, he assisted people—whether they were farmers, poets, or students—by providing help with interpretation and understanding. If there were a chasm to be crossed or a gap in understanding, one would hope to find a *hermaion*, a messenger of the gods who would provide wisdom or insight. Too often, we rely on Hermes when we read our Bibles! The dominant school of thought teaches that we find meaning in our Bibles in the knowing, the interpretation, and the special guides. This is not wrong, but it is incomplete.

When we pursue meaning, we must weigh the cost of our methods. Remember what happened to the frog in high school science class? It entered the class croaking and jumping, full of life. But then it was studied scientifically. Pinned down on a board and cut open. We learned what its heart and liver looked like. Things once hidden were now in plain sight. In the process, something important was lost—the frog's life!

In the same way, we must be careful when we study the *living* word of God. I am grateful for hermeneutics. There is much to be gained by doing the hard work of understanding original languages, historical backgrounds, and ancient cultures. As one entrusted to teach the word of God, I take this seriously. So I'm not advocating that we reject the art and science of biblical interpretation. Rather, I want to bring the *art* side into the picture to bring balance.

The Scriptures are a mystery being revealed, a song being sung, a way of life being presented. They are meant to be sought and experienced and lived. They are more than a science project.

So there needs to be a way to know them without reducing them to manageable portions for our finite minds, right? *What if we experienced the word of God as a song that sets us free to compose, a melody that has room for our voices to join in with the ancients?*

Jazz theology is a participation in the basic patterns revealed in biblical life situations. It inquires not only what God did and said but how he said and did it. Furthermore, it expects him to do it again in a similar way in our lives ... just as jazz musicians improvise new music and enliven old songs.

Carl Ellis, author and professor

German goldsmith and printer Johannes Gensfleisch zur Laden zum Gutenberg (how's that for a name!) created the printing press in the mid-1400s. He then printed the Gutenberg Bible. Though there were fewer than two hundred copies produced, this event launched a new era in Bible reading. Gutenberg's innovation ushered in the possibility of everyone, not just the privileged, having their own copy of the Scriptures. While it didn't happen overnight, we now live in a day where we give Bibles away, free of charge. We have Gutenberg to thank. Now virtually anyone can have a Bible in their hands in the language of their choice. We can store the Scriptures digitally on our computer or have them read to us as we drive down the street. No longer are we at the mercy of someone else telling us what the Bible says, as all of us can study it for ourselves. For the most part this is a good thing

The Gutenberg press also introduced us to a new way of reading the Bible—in isolation. The "personal quiet time" was invented. Now that everyone has a copy, you no longer need to read it with others. We still gather together for sermons and Bible studies, but it's not the way it was pre–printing press.

When there weren't enough copies of the Scriptures to go around, people would come together for worship and a priest would read portions from the Old Testament, an epistle, and a gospel. He then needed a way to help everyone remember the Scriptures, so he took string with beads, and each bead stood for the Scripture of the day (this would eventually become the rosary). That was it. You had the groove, the basic melody, and then over the next week as you worked your fields you also worked the word of God into your mind, internalizing it until it came out in your everyday life. What mattered most was not if you "knew it" chapter and verse but if you "knew it" as you lived it. After all, mere theological knowledge is not what it's all about.[1] Isn't it interesting that a large number of the classic books about the spiritual life were written during a time when not everyone had a Bible? What did they know? How did they know? Reading the Bible with a jazz sensibility means that we expect to enter and participate in the world of Scripture.

Jazzaneutics

The last thing I want you to hear me say is that I'm against classical hermeneutics. That's not the case. Rather, I'm proposing an accompaniment that will put the "art" back into the "art and science of biblical interpretation." A jazz-shaped approach to the Scriptures emphasizes knowing them by living them in community. It's not just reading our Bibles but letting the Bible read us. Instead of always interpreting the word of God, we desire more that *it* interpret *us*.

We need an alternative, complementary way of knowing God's word. What I'm talking about is an approach to the Scriptures that sees the meaning in the knowing *and* the doing—knowing *by* doing.

As we've seen, jazz is an interpretive art. The goal is to be so familiar with the originals that we can then add our own voice within the "bounds and bonds of the song" as Ossie Davis said.[2] The goal of "jazzaneutics" (if you will) is similar. We should spend so much time in meditation and memorization of the Scriptures that when called on, we—like Stephen and Mary of old— can play them like a song from the heart.

When we read our Bibles, the meaning is not only in what the original authors are saying but also in what they are doing. For if the main point of the Scriptures is primarily in what is being said, then we only need to understand the words. However, if there is more to be learned than that, then we need another—not better, but *additional*—way of approaching the word of God, namely, knowing by doing.

What I'm talking about is syncopation and improvisation. When we find our voice, we are accenting different beats in God's word and playing off of them in a way that honors them and inspires us not to see hidden meaning but to see meaning in a personal way.

Hermeneutics shows us that we should begin by asking questions that help us find meaning in our Bibles: What was the author saying? What is the original context? What do I need to know about the original readers and their historical setting that will help me understand what is being said?

A jazz-shaped approach pushes us further. After we gain answers to the above questions, we draw on our key notes and ask, What is the author doing? Can I syncopate it? Can I improvise on what I'm hearing? In order to fully grasp what I'm trying to say, you need to commit to some time in the woodshed. So grab your Bible, and let's go!

What Is the Author Doing?

Classical hermeneutics examines what the author is saying. Jazzaneutics goes a step further and asks, What is the author *doing*?

To see what I mean, skim Nehemiah 1 or Daniel 9. In each of these passages, we see two men of God confessing not their own sins but the sins of their people. What does it mean to know these passages? Is it to have a cognitive understanding of them — to know who Nehemiah was praying for and what sins Daniel was referring to? Should we also *do* what these men are doing? Should we wrestle with concepts of corporate confession? Should we ask questions such as, "Who are my people?" and "How do we confess our sins?"

A jazzaneutic approach will push us toward a "knowing by doing." We don't simply recognize that Nehemiah and Daniel confessed the sins of their people, but we ask, "When was the last time I confessed the sins of my people?"

Or take Acts 17:16–34, where Paul presents the gospel by connecting it to the poetry, spirituality, and philosophy of Athens — all without quoting Scripture. There is much to be learned from what is being said in this passage, but shouldn't we also be able to do what Paul did?

Or reread Stephen's speech in Acts 7. What was

he actually *doing*? He was explaining the redemptive works of God through the actual history of his people. Carl Ellis draws our attention to this need: "It is a disgrace that we have not learned to preach 'the full counsel of God' through our history, the way Stephen and later Paul were able to preach through Jewish history."[3]

Jesus' parable of the soils is compelling and seems rather straightforward. Four different soils each receive seed with vastly different outcomes. But take time to really read Jesus' explanation of the parable.[4] What was Jesus *doing*? Why did he interpret it the way he did? This is the only parable that Jesus unpacks for us, and it makes me wonder, Is he showing us the way to now go back and read his other parables?

Do we know our Bibles by knowing what they say or by doing what they do? Jazz says we *don't know* until we *can do*. This leads us to syncopation and ultimately improvisation.

Syncopating the Scriptures

Remember, syncopation is accenting the offbeat and exploring the tension. We can do this with the Scriptures. It isn't that there is hidden meaning or mysterious codes in our Bibles. No, but there is meaning that is often missed because of the questions we ask. If we ask questions that have to do with the intellectual meaning of the text, then we will arrive at one set of answers. If we ask questions that have to do with living the Scriptures, then we will arrive at another set of answers. Both types of questions are needed.

Look at what happens when we search for the off-beat in the gospel of John—which we find by first identifying the main beats. One of the main beats that John built in to the telling of the life of Jesus was the "I am" statements of Jesus. When you read John's gospel all the way through, you begin to see it; you even begin to anticipate it. Jesus' use of the title "I am" and John's placement of the phrase in his twenty-one chapters are similar to a drummer's keeping us on beat:

I am the bread of life (6:35, 48).

I am the light of the world (8:12; 9:5).

I am the gate (10:9).

I am the good shepherd (10:11).

I am the resurrection and the life (11:25).

I am the way and the truth and the life (14:6)

I am the true vine (15:1).

We usually read these and only hear the main beat. And if that is all we know, we will be eternally enriched. Each of these statements reveals who Jesus desires to be to us. If Jesus is the "I am," then we are to recall Moses and the burning bush.[5] If he is the "bread of life," then Jesus is our manna.[6] If we are to see Jesus as the "light of the world," then he desires that we understand the Feast of Tabernacles and the role that candles and light play in that Jewish feast.[7]

But there is more to be discovered if we syncopate the Scriptures.

In addition to the main driving beat of the "I ams," there is also an offbeat to John's gospel. It isn't hidden (Jesus actually points it out), but it does require that we do some extra work to see it. It's worth it though, because with each statement our Savior was telling us something not only about himself but about his Father and ourselves as well.

Jesus set the groove with the basic beat—"I am ... I am ... I am"—each time finishing it with a revelation about himself. Then he adds a surprise on his final use of the phrase in John 15. First he says, "I am the true vine, and my Father is the gardener." That's more information about himself, just like the other "I ams." But this time he added an unexpected beat and gave us information about his Father (he's the gardener). Before we are able to fully comprehend, he syncopates the beat again. "I am the vine; you are the branches." This time he gives information about us (we are branches).

Do you see the implications?

In those two statements, Jesus reveals the offbeat of his "I am" sayings. Up until this point in the gospel of John, the "I am" formula was revealing something about Jesus only. But in these last two instances, Jesus shows us that each statement also has the potential to reveal more of our identity and our heavenly Father's identity.

This should send us back to all the other statements to ask two questions:

What does this say about the Father?

What does this say about me?

Knowing Jesus as the "I am" reveals more of the Father's identity. It also shows our identity in Christ and our relationship to the Father.

You'll want to go back through the "I ams" yourself, but let me get you started. In John 6:35, Jesus said, "I am the bread of life." He was telling us something about his Father: He is the provider of bread—the baker, if you will. But Jesus was also revealing a hard truth about us: we are hungry and unsatisfied without real food. We need him.

I'll let you enjoy syncopating the rest on your own ...

Improvising the Scriptures

When a conductor waves the baton and the classical orchestra comes to life, the goal is to reproduce the composer's music as it is written. This is good and beautiful. Jazz has a different goal. Once the original composition is internalized, it seeks not to imitate but to improvise. Which makes me wonder: Can we do what the writers of Scripture did?

Let me warn you, what I'm about to say may sound a little strange. You may even ask if you are allowed to do what I'm suggesting. So before we go any further, let me assure you I believe that the Scriptures are complete and that we do not need to add to them. This isn't what I'm suggesting here. Rather, I want to note that the Scriptures are comprised of a variety of types of literature. They contain prayers, letters, poetry, and history, to name a few genres. Can we write history or poetry the way the biblical writers did? I think so. As I said, I know we cannot add to Scripture; rather, Scripture can inspire and teach us how to compose so that others can see the good news that God is bringing forth in our lives.

Psalm 23 is a good place to start. Written by King David and rich in metaphor, this ancient psalm has comforted many through suffering and the passage into death. Starting out, we should seek to understand all the ins and outs of the sheep business — the lives of shepherds in the ancient Near East. This will allow us to experience God as our Good and Great Shepherd who has our best interest at heart. That's classical hermeneutics.

But what if we were to do what David was doing? Have you ever tried to write your own Psalm 23?

Think about it. David's vocation was that of a shepherd. As he spent long, lonely nights and boring days watching over the sheep, he had a lot of time on his hands—and what is clear is that he used it to write poetry about his God. Can you envision how Psalm 23 came about? One day, David began to make a comparison between what he did for helpless sheep and what God did for him. "The Lord is my shepherd..."

And with that he was off. His job as a shepherd was now a metaphor for his spiritual life.

Can you and I do this? Yes, and when we do, it's called improvisation. Try it. Take your vocation and see it as a unique way of talking about your relationship with God.

How would yours begin?

"The Lord is my ..."

Here are two beautiful examples from some friends of mine.

The Twenty-third Psalm of an Accountant

Cheryl Baumbach[8]

Lord, you are my accountant,
You care about the details.
Every event of my life is recorded double-entry,
A debit and credit on earth and up in heaven.

For while I may see the cash or visible fixed assets,
You are posting the liability or expense.
When I am burdened by debt or the cost,
You record the eternal investment.

Too often I am overwhelmed with paperwork piling
   up, my to-do list ever growing,
But at those times you beckon me to the
   mountainside
To gain perspective and strategize my efforts.

And when all of life seems out of balance,
You give me wisdom to reconcile the variance
If I just seek your face.

Lord, help me understand my financial statement,
To know the numbers are only part of the story.
For at the bottom is reflected the blood equity you
   alone could provide,
Captioned by two simple words—Net Worth.

The Twenty-third Psalm
of a Motorcycle Mechanic

Jon Paul[9]

The Lord is my motorcycle mechanic;
there is nothing that I lack.
On safe roads you let me travel;
with fresh fuel and clean oil you fill me.
You restore my state of tune,
you repair all of the unsound modifications
I have let others perform on me,
you repair what others deemed un-repairable and
    hopeless.
You guide me along the right path for the sake of
    your name.
Even though I travel down the dark, unsafe, and
    potholed alleyway, I fear no harm
because I know you are my owner and driver;
your fine tooling and loving hands give me
surefootedness and steadfastness.

You set out an open lift and your toolbox before me,
even as my abusers watch impatiently through the
    waiting room window,
eager for their chance to try to run me into the
    ground once again.

> You restore my timing and set it in sync
> with your service manual specifications,
> not with my own misadjusted ways.
> My fuel is topped off and refilled by you.
> Only your Goodness, Love, and all-perfect
>   Knowledge
> will repair me, renew me, and bring me back to your
>   intended original design,
> even as my odometer has counted off hundreds of
>   thousands of miles through my life.
> I will dwell in the garage of the Lord, in your service
>   bay,
> for you are my chosen mechanic and my builder.
> You will give me all the maintenance, repair, and
>   soundness
> for the millions of miles to come.

Do you see it? The word of God sets us free to compose; it is a melody that has room for our voices to join in with the ancients.

We can do the same thing with the Gospels. A gospel is a unique form of autobiography. Matthew, Mark, and John were writing their eyewitness accounts of Jesus Christ. Luke, who had never met Jesus, conducted a series of interviews.[10] He likely interviewed

Mary, Elizabeth, Lazarus, and the lepers. Because of the work of the gospel writers, we have actual encounters with Jesus recorded for us to read.

Have you had an actual encounter with Jesus? Has someone else told you about their encounter? If you choose to write these things down, you have started a gospel. Again, I'm not saying that we try to write Scripture but that we allow the Bible to show us new ways of reaching out to others. The four gospels show us another way of telling our stories as God's story. The disciples recorded their life events from the perspective of encounters with Jesus. What mattered most to them was not what happened to them but how their experiences revealed Jesus. They were students of the words and deeds of Jesus. We can learn from them.

> Improvisation is expressing who I am within the bounds and bonds of the song.
>
> **Ossie Davis, actor, director, and playwright**

I have a journal that is reserved for firsthand God-sightings. I write in it when I have a personal encounter with the risen Lord or hear about someone else's. I began "my gospel" a few years ago by making a list of all the times Jesus was real to me in my life. I add to it occasionally. It's not a masterpiece, but it is true and real. It's good news!

Improvising the Scriptures means that we have

so familiarized ourselves with the eternal melody of God that we now can play off of it. The possibilities are endless, and you will begin to see them in normal, everyday life.

As we look at anthills in our backyards, we remember how the writer of Proverbs drew spiritual meaning from these little creatures.[11] Improvising, we begin to look at spiders and sparrows with new eyes. As we write notes and emails, we can do so with greater expectations as we remember how the apostle Paul wrote letters (epistles) and inspired others to faithfulness.

Let me ask the question again: *What if we experienced the word of God as a song that sets us free to compose, a melody that has room for our voices to join in with the ancients?* I hope you now see a way for this to happen through syncopation and improvisation. In these ways, the Scriptures come to life. Better yet, they bring *us* to life. It's not hard to believe that our Bibles are a beautiful melody. What is difficult to grasp is that they have room for our voices.

Whose Are We?

When my son Gabriel was six years old, he walked up to me wearing his suit. This seemed a little odd, given that we had no plans to leave the house. He said,

"People say I look like you." He then asked, "Can we read the Bible?"

As we sat down together to read, the tone of his voice hinted that something deeper was going on, so I asked him, "What are you feeling?"

He said, "I'm feeling like I want to be somebody."

I almost cried.

I have felt that same ache, that deep desire to be who God has made me to be. I remember how my Father in heaven made his presence known to me at a young age. And now I am watching the Spirit at work in my son's life. That moment captures what it means to be made in the image of God. We want to be somebody. We know — somewhere deep inside — that we are somebody. We need God and his word. We also need an audience. The street musician wanted to be somebody. That's why he came out of the woodshed and onto the streets to find an audience so that he could reap the benefits of call-and-response.

God is calling. I've learned that this is the beginning of meaning. The fact that there is One who calls out to me means that I now matter. He calls us to himself. That's why the ultimate question is not "Who are we?" but "Whose are we?" This creates yearning. Now that we know we are somebody because of whose we are, we want to become that somebody so we can "take hold of that for which Christ Jesus took hold of

[us]."[12] So we begin to practice in the presence of others, calling out, hoping that others will respond.

When you are trying to find your voice, you are looking for composition. Not to compose but rather to be composed. You sense you are more like an instrument than a musician. You desire to live a composed life. To be a woodwind instrument that the Spirit of God is blowing through so that the notes you play are chosen for you. Even if you become a one-note wonder, all that matters is that it is the note composed for you by your Creator.

As you look for composition, remember that others are doing the same. Is there anyone practicing around you? Calling with the hope of a response? *If you hear the sound of someone practicing, follow the sound. They need you.*

Searching for a Composed Life

I remember how it happened for me. I asked my grandmother for a Bible shortly after I gave my life to Christ at the age of nine. The Bible she gave me was an NIV Thompson Chain, and it is still the one I read devotionally today. I wish I could remember why, but the first book of the Bible that I read was James. It was here that I gained my understanding of faith with feet—the fact that what we believe needs to connect with real-life

problems such as social class and poverty. And then
for some reason, I turned to the book of Revelation.
All I can say is that at the age of nine, it literally scared
the hell out of me! After that, I stopped reading the
Scriptures for a few months. However, I couldn't stay
away for long, for those words spoke to me. I made a
decision to read the whole Bible. It took me a couple
of years, and much of it I didn't understand, but I was
enthralled with it. I made notes in the margins, looked
up the cross-references, and—over time—began to
understand how it was put together. I would read my
Bible in the morning and take it with me to school to
get a glimpse at lunchtime. At night I would read it in
my room, often falling asleep with it in my hands.

For a little boy who didn't know who his daddy
was, the Scriptures captivated me. They became my
lifeline because in them my True Father spoke to me.

Before we can improvise and syncopate, we must
learn the scales of the faith. Those early years were for
me a time of learning the basic chords and structures
of Scripture. It was a season of noticing the nuances.
By the time I was sixteen, I had read through the
Scriptures a few times and listened intently with pen
in hand to as many sermons as possible. I was ready
to start experimenting, risking, and searching for my
own voice.

When I was a freshman in high school, I thought I

was going to be an orthopedic surgeon. I even enrolled in Latin class because someone told me that medical terms were derived from that "dead" language. One day, I broke a bone in my foot during cross-country practice and wound up in a cast—for eight months! I saw this as the will of God for my life. Here I wanted to be an orthopedic surgeon, and now I had the opportunity to watch one up close working on my body. The Lord was indeed at work—but not as I suspected. It was during this time of impaired mobility, as I lay with my leg propped up in my bed and my Bible on my lap, that the Spirit of Christ spoke to me and called me to be a pastor.

Within days of this holy moment, I told my pastor about what the Lord had told me. We prayed. He asked me if I would like to preach my first sermon at the Wednesday night prayer meeting. I said yes.

As I walked home from the meeting with my pastor, I panicked! What had I just committed to? Me, *preach*? What would I say? After all, I knew what the Scriptures said, but what were they supposed to say through me?

That was the day I began to experience community as a jam session in which the Holy Spirit, the Scriptures, a mentor, and an audience help to call out one's voice.

I prayed, studied, and suffered through a few anxiety attacks trying to figure out what to say. Then, through an odd set of circumstances, I happened upon an idea—donkeys. I would talk about the donkeys of the Bible and draw application from their lives to ours. I'll save the details of my first sermon for another conversation. The point here is that my pastor helped me. The twenty or so people at the prayer meeting loved me and spoke into my life, even after I called them a bunch of burros! I was beginning to find my voice.

My pastor's name was Ron Johnson. He walked with me. I watched him. We took car rides together and talked ministry. He let me preach at more Wednesday night prayer meetings. Then Sunday night services. Finally, the big game—Sunday morning!

I was one of only a handful of African-Americans in this all-white church. Many people of this congregation were encouraging and loving toward me. I only found out a few years ago that while my pastor was mentoring me, he and his family were receiving threats on their safety because of their commitment to me. Today, Ron Johnson and his wife, Nancy, sit in the congregation every Sunday morning as I have the privilege to proclaim the words of God. Ron is not a pastor anymore (not officially, that is). And I am forever grateful to this man for helping me find my voice.

He seems to be happy to have played his role.

developing your ear

*What if every moment of life
with Christ is pregnant with promise —
containing the potential to be
a one-of-a-kind masterpiece?*

If I could use only one word to define the essence of
jazz, it would be *listening*. Given the improvisational
nature of jazz at any moment, a fellow ensemble member may do something they have never done before, and
the rest of the group needs to not just be playing the
song but *listening* to the song as it unfolds. Jazz is about
having our ear tuned in to those around us so that we
don't miss out on what they are doing. Listening is important because no moment is "just" a moment.

I discovered this a few years ago, when Rosa Parks

visited our church. She was standing in the lobby with about twenty other people when she said, "I'm tired; could I take a seat?" She said it so softly that everyone missed it. If I hadn't been standing right next to her, I, too, would have missed it. Because no one else reacted, I began to question if I had really heard what I thought I heard. I was too intimidated to ask her to repeat herself, so I just trusted my ear and went searching for a chair. With none nearby, I ran all over, looking for the perfect one. At first all I found were those metal folding kind; I eventually grabbed one of the semi-cushy —comfortable looking, yet not really—chairs from the waiting area of the office. It was the best I could do.

I carried it to her and said, "Ma'am, here's a seat." She said thank you in her quiet, almost indiscernible voice. I couldn't believe it; I gave a seat to the woman who had stayed in her seat. What a privilege! What a moment!

Is It the *Ubuntu* of America?

The archbishop Desmond Tutu has taught the world about the *ubuntu* way of life in South Africa—the idea that a person becomes a person through other people. In parts of Africa, "Hello" is replaced with "*Sawu bona*," which means, "I see you." The reply is, "*Sikhona*"—"I am here." One author comments, "The order of the exchange is important: until you see me, I do not exist. It's as if, when you see me, you bring me into existence."[1]

Some South African churches have a meaningful way to welcome new members. They break a clay pot and give a piece of it to everyone in the church family, including the new person. Each individual is to bring their piece back the following week so that they can reassemble the broken vessel. It is a symbol of what is necessary for kingdom community in that culture. It is their way of saying, "I see you." I see that you are here, and I am making room for you. I see when you are missing, for there is a void where your piece belongs.

> The most important thing I look for in a musician is whether he knows how to listen.
> **Duke Ellington, composer, pianist, and bandleader**

Could jazz be the *ubuntu* of America?

In the United States I don't think we are wondering if someone sees us. Our culture is different, and so our questions are different. We are the land of democracy, the place where everyone has a voice and a vote. In *ubuntu* it is, "I see you." In jazz it is, "I hear you." We wonder, Do you hear me? Do you know that I have something to say? The gospel gives us new ears to hear God and one another. This is where jazz helps us, because it is all about listening. It is about hearing what each person has to offer. It is about you playing your solo and then me playing mine. It is about us playing together with breaks for individual contributions and joining the triune ensemble-God who is one and yet allows for our contributions.

Jazz just might be the *ubuntu* of America.

Incarnation: Having Time to Listen to Others

Jazz is listening to the tone and timing of the words of those around us. One of the greatest gifts we can give to another human being is to not be so wrapped up in what we are going to say but to really tune in to what *others* are saying. The practice of listening surely can take the pressure off in a room full of people. Instead of constantly trying to be interesting, all we need to be is *interested*.

Jesus said that we should love each other as he loved us.[2] He demonstrated the meaning of this kind of love when he washed his disciple's feet. It was such a beautiful display of grace as he knelt before Judas, even though Judas would betray him minutes later. He knelt before the others, though they would all turn from him before the night would end. Yet he loved each one of them. Sin is "what turns us away from love."[3] All of us want to be loving people; the question is, Do we want to love like Jesus loved? Wanting to love and taking advantage of a moment to love are often divided by an uncrossable chasm of convenience and time constraints.

The One Who Loves Is the One Who Serves

Jesus shows us that love requires stooping in the presence of others. It requires a humility that allows us to be aware of what the moment is presenting. In the Scriptures, before Jesus was known as Savior, he was revealed as the Servant.[4] That is, when Isaiah proclaimed the coming of the Anointed One, he spoke of him in terms of the Supreme Stooper. So it should come as no surprise that when Jesus decided to show "the full extent of his love," he served.[5] I am convinced that if we want to truly live out the gospel in our world in a compelling way, it is going to require that we out-serve others.

The One Who Serves Is the One Who Listens

I have a friend who was visiting an elderly home-bound gentleman. As he let himself into the older man's house, my friend asked, "How are you doing?" The man quietly responded, "I think I messed myself." My friend had a choice to make in the moment. To listen or not. To serve or not. To love or not. I will not go into the graphic details of how my friend managed to get the three-hundred-pound man into the shower and cleaned him up. But I will say this: we have moments to be Jesus to people if we are willing to listen.

Serving is all about identifying and meeting needs.[6] That's what Jesus did for his disciples. Jesus was able to serve them because he was listening to them — yes, as they argued. That's what they were doing right before they entered the upper room. They were debating greatness. None of them were going to stoop down and help wash anybody else's feet. Jesus loved. Jesus served. Jesus listened. If we want to be like Jesus, then we would do well to keep lists of the needs of those around us, whether they are our neighbors, church friends, enemies, or the teachers and students at the local public school. Our ability to be supreme servants is directly linked to how well we have developed our ear for the needs of others and the still, small voice of our God. Listening is a lost art, though James, the brother of Jesus, taught us that our ears should stay ahead of our mouths.[7]

Jesus' birth was utterly unique. As an eternal being, he is the only person whose birth was not his beginning. The Incarnation is one of those mysteries that leave us able to apprehend the magnificence of our Lord even though we cannot fully comprehend it with our finite minds. What is clear is that Jesus' incarnation is a model for how to love — not from a distance but up close, in the flesh, close enough to truly hear the needs of our neighbors.

Sometimes the first step is as simple as reading a book. Recently I reread *Black Like Me*. Years had passed since I first followed John Howard Griffin's amazing journey of a white man living as a black man in the Deep South in the late 1950s. He drew his title from the closing lines of jazz poet Langston Hughes's poem "Dream Variations": *Night coming tenderly / Black like me.*

In his amazing saga, Griffin decided to discover for himself what it was actually like to live as a black man in America — to listen incarnationally. Aided by medication and sunlamps, he darkened his skin. With shaved head he set out on a spectacular journey into the land of lynching, segregation, and oppression. Griffin offers us a tale of courage, honesty, and cruelty from a perspective that most Americans can only dream about. He models listening in the way of the incarnation. Griffin was able to speak to the problem of race

> It was telling a story. If you listen to jazz, then every jazz musician has a story to tell. And he tells it. This is why to follow jazz you have to really listen because everybody is telling a story.
>
> **Buck O'Neil, Negro League baseball player**

in America because he was willing to become one with the oppressed in order to speak prophetically on their behalf. I admire this man who chose to experience a foreign pain and struggle. I am challenged by him because he became "black like me."

There is a reason jazz musicians will choose to learn to play other instruments; it allows them to support and listen better from the perspective of those around them. I want to learn how to follow in the steps of the incarnate Christ. I want to be willing to read the books, to see the movies, to drive in the car for six hours until I reach the desolate reservation of our nation's Natives. Or simply to walk down the street and talk with the sad-faced man who was arrested last month ... to mourn with my gay neighbor who just lost his father ... to grieve with the woman across the street whose husband just abandoned her.

To listen.

Incarnation: having time to listen to others (with towel in hand).

Resurrection: Having Time to Listen to God

Core to the gospel is a Christ who not only suffered and died but also rose from the dead. And so Jesus reserves the right to break into our lives at any moment. Jesus' resurrection means that we live life on the edge of our seats, for every moment possesses the possibility of an encounter with him.

Mary Magdalene's eyes were filled with tears from the dual shock of Jesus' not being in the tomb and her glimpse of angels: "She turned around and saw Jesus standing there, but she did not realize that it was Jesus."[8] He called her "woman," and she thought he was the gardener—but it was he, the risen Christ. Christ incognito, possible only because he has risen. The other disciples told Thomas about their moments with Jesus, but he wanted some too. A week passed, and the disciples were having dinner, and "though the doors were locked, Jesus came and stood among them"—just another moment in which Christ was incognito.[9] Peter went back to his life of fishing. "Early in the morning, Jesus stood on the shore, but the disciples did not realize that it was Jesus."[10] Recognition eventually came, and then a moment followed in which Peter told Jesus that he loved him—and then again and yet again. Once for each time that Peter had disowned him on the night of his arrest. Or who can forget the two unnamed travelers on the road to Emmaus? The same day that Jesus rose from the dead, these two were walking and talking when "Jesus himself came up and walked along with them; but they were kept from recognizing him."[11]

Christ is risen! He is risen indeed! Therefore, every

moment of life is a moment in which Jesus himself can
—and might—make himself known to you and me.
The Lord is near—even right now.[12] When the apostle
Paul wrote about the importance of the resurrection,
he included these moments as part of his reasoning.

> For what I received I passed on to you as of first
> importance: that Christ died for our sins accord-
> ing to the Scriptures, that he was buried, that he
> was raised on the third day according to the Scrip-
> tures, and that he appeared to Peter, and then to
> the Twelve. After that, he appeared to more than
> five hundred of the brothers at the same time,
> most of whom are still living, though some have
> fallen asleep. Then he appeared to James, then to
> all the apostles, and last of all he appeared to me
> also, as to one abnormally born.[13]

*Christ is alive. Lord, help us to listen. If you were to
come and stand next to us in your resurrected glory, we
would be able to see and hear you—but you are not here.
Lord, help us to hear your Spirit.*

We live in the age of the Spirit. Christ not only
rose from the dead, but he also ascended into heaven,
ushering in a better way—life in the Spirit. If you
have ever watched five-year-olds play soccer, then you
can understand why Jesus said, "It is for your good
that I am going away. Unless I go away, the Coun-

selor will not come to you; but if I go, I will send him to you."[14] From the moment the whistle blows to commence a children's soccer game, each player abandons their position and goes wherever the ball is. For the next hour, all you see is this mass of bodies bunched together around the ball. If Jesus hadn't left after his resurrection, this would be the state of our Christian life. If Jesus were physically on earth, who would ever leave his presence? We would just follow him en masse, like little kids around a soccer ball. Instead, Jesus went up, the Spirit came down, and the church went out. We are able to spread out and go into the entire world precisely because the risen Lord left us behind. Resurrection living—that is, life in the Spirit—requires that we develop our ear so that we can discern the still, small voice of our risen King and respond to his call.

My first impression one particular Sunday morning was that numbers were down. The unusually low temperatures we were experiencing in the Mile High City seemed to have kept a number of folks at home.

As we were about to begin the service, an usher informed me that a man was there who had just lost his wife a few days ago. I sought him out, making my way down the somewhat crowded pew. When he saw me, he came undone. As the congregation sang, he and I prayed and wept. The last song of the worship set was almost finished, and I had to make my way to the platform. I tried to stay on script with the announcements, but all I could think of was Henry's broken heart. So I stopped and told everyone about his pain and how when one of us is hurt, all of us are wounded. Those sitting around him laid hands on him, and we all prayed. Our worship leader began singing, "It Is Well."

We cried collectively.

The Spirit then prompted me to talk about heaven, the cross, and the love of God. When I finished, everyone bowed their heads, and I invited anyone who had never given his or her life to Christ to do so, to seek him in that moment. I will never forget the twenty or so hands that were lifted high when I asked if anyone had just received Christ for the first time.

> Jazz is primarily a heard reality.
>
> Kirk Byron Jones, professor of ethics and preaching

I am amazed at our God! I saw a service with a low turnout because of cold temperatures; he saw a man mourning the death of his wife and hearts that were receptive to the gospel.

Incarnation: having time to listen to others (with towel in hand).

Resurrection: having time to listen to God.

Do you notice the huge assumption of listening? *We must have time!*

Do You Have Time, or Does Time Have You?

Jazz musicians have time to listen. One saxophonist I know finishes his solo and then sits down on the floor and watches his fellow performers take their turn. It is a sign of respect for their ability, but he is also listening for what they are doing in case he can adjust when it is his turn. He's the star whom everyone in the audience has paid to see, but during the performance he takes the time to listen to everyone else.

We are consumed with time—which can be one of the greatest enemies of grace in our lives. When I ask, "How is your prayer life?" time often becomes the sole criterion for evaluating the quality of our communion with the Lord. We measure the value of our relationship with God in terms of time.

We measure it in minutes, not moments.

Time is even assumed in the way we ask about our relationship to God. "How is your quiet TIME?" We then answer accordingly, based on how much time we spent today versus yesterday. We strive to find the elusive "Sweet Hour of Prayer."

Consequently, we don't have time; *time has us.*

The biblical vision of prayer has a different starting point. It's not, "How much did I pray today?" but rather, "Did I ever stop praying today?" Our preoccupation with time leaves us missing the point of unceasing prayer.[15] In the process we strive for bare minimums instead of pursuing what is truly possible, namely, unending, unbroken communion with Jesus. We were designed to live with God for all time, for God is with us all of the time.

But when time has us, grace is suffocated.

The Pharisees committed the "heresy of exactness,"[16] and Jesus pronounced "woes" on them because of it. They consumed themselves with measuring and calculating their faith to the point that they missed God in the process. Even more, the people they led felt unworthy of God's love because they could never measure up.

Do you have time, or does time have you? Time is important because of the moments it possesses. We will miss these moments if we have the wrong view of time. It's no wonder that we overreact to the tyranny of time by "killing time" or "just doing time." As author Os Guinness observes, "The ticktock of the clock has become the background drumbeat and staccato bark of the drill sergeant who drives us across the parade ground of life."[17] There is a jazz way to keep time so that we have time and time doesn't have us.

Swing: Becoming Timekeepers

In a jazz ensemble, the drummer is the timekeeper. He sits obscurely in the back, ever keeping the beat, driving the tempo, and signaling timing changes. His job is to *keep time* in a way that sets the others free. He listens and responds to the moments and in the process keeps time for all. He has the worst seat in the house. Think about it; as he sits in the back all he sees are the backsides of his fellow musicians. It's not a great place to see, *but it's a great place to serve*. Perched in the back he is able to react to what others are doing. He is able to listen and respond by keeping time so that any moment can burst forth. For drummers, time is flexible, and different drummers keep time differently, even while they are playing in the same time.

The essence of jazz is listening.

If we are going to experience a jazz-shaped faith, then we must have time instead of letting time have us. Having time allows us to live incarnationally and in anticipation of a resurrected Christ. A drummer has time and plays with it for the purpose of the moment. Swinging for the sake of those who have something to say. As jazz musician Ornette Coleman once said, "When the band is playing with the drummer, it's rock and roll, but when the drummer is playing with the band, it's jazz."[18] Timekeepers have time. Having time affords the opportunity to listen. Have you developed your ear?

The Acoustics of Listening

Tone deafness is the audio version of color blindness. Just as some look at a mosaic of colors and can't distinguish the red from the blue, so too some can't hear the differences in tone. We don't need to worry, however, about tone deafness in our relationship with God. Jesus told us that "his sheep follow him because they know his voice. But they will never follow a stranger; in fact, they will run away from him because they do not recognize a stranger's voice."[19]

We can and should be able to discern the voice of the Good Shepherd. Hearing God should be the reality for his sheep. But hearing God's voice is as difficult as truly hearing each other. It's easier said than done. Eugene Peterson, in his book *Working the Angles*, says there are three stories for which we are developing our ear — first, the story of what God has said to those in the past (the Bible); second, the story of what God is saying to us; finally, the story of what God is saying to those around us. Every person we encounter is someone who is also on the verge of encountering Christ incognito. At any moment God might make his presence known to them. The Spirit is even speaking to those who don't know God.[20] If we have time, then we can help others respond to the call of God, serving them as a drummer serves while nestled in the back.

Samuel needed help recognizing the voice of God. The Lord called Samuel's name, but the boy thought that it was Eli calling. Each time he heard the voice, Samuel mistakenly went to Eli because, "Samuel did not yet know the Lord: The word of the Lord had not yet been revealed to him."[21] Samuel's ear was undeveloped.

> The Lord called Samuel a third time, and Samuel got up and went to Eli and said, "Here I am; you called me."
>
> Then Eli realized that the Lord was calling the boy. So Eli told Samuel, "Go and lie down, and if he calls you, say, 'Speak, Lord, for your servant is listening.'" So Samuel went and lay down in his place.
>
> The Lord came and stood there, calling as at the other times, "Samuel! Samuel!"
>
> Then Samuel said, "Speak, for your servant is listening."[22]

When we develop our ear, it's not only so we can gain a benefit but also so that we can have the ministry of Eli to those in our ensemble. Dallas Willard explains:

How wonderful that Eli recognized what was happening to young Samuel and could tell him what to do to begin his lifelong conversational walk with God! It might well have been years, in the prevailing circumstances, before Samuel would have found his way. We must not foolishly assume that, if God speaks, one automatically knows what is happening and who is talking. If Samuel did not know, surely many others also will not know.[23]

Those around us need us as much as we need them.

Develop Your Ear

Jazz employs a number of disciplines to develop our ears, and these disciplines can help us develop our spiritual ears so we can listen to God more intently and listen to the needs of others more specifically.

The Break: Jazz incorporates this technique to make it easier to listen to a particular person. It is the practice of creating space in a musical piece by having all or most of the band members stop playing in order to create a break in the music. The moments are planned, but what happens in them is up to the soloist.

This technique of stopping everything so that everyone can listen to one person more clearly is similar to what the ancient Hebrews called *Selah*. Remember,

Selah is the little word you see throughout the book of Psalms. While no one knows for sure, it appears to be a musical notation to the singers that something was supposed to happen at that point in the song. Most scholars think it means to pause—*to take a break*—during the song. One theory asserts that it was a signal to ring a bell. When this happened in the worship service, all were to pause and listen until the bell had been fully rung. It was a signal to be silent and—even when you couldn't hear the bell but it was still vibrating—to keep listening. It was space for God to solo.

Perhaps the reason God introduced the concept of Sabbath was so we would have regular breaks to listen. Sabbath and *Selah* are preplanned moments where we *have time to listen*. They are breaks in the cacophony of our lives.

Dictation: Dictation is a tool used by musicians to develop their ear. It is the process of listening to a piece of music note by note and transcribing it to paper. A jazz musician will often listen to the solo of another musician who plays the same instrument and then attempt to dictate the notes being played.

Tone matching: Tone matching, which is similar to dictation, is the practice of getting together with another musician and playing what the other person plays as closely as possible. I know of a very accomplished bass player who taught himself to play by sitting on his couch with his instrument and playing the bass line of whatever music happened to be playing on TV.

These last two techniques are about learning to listen, not only to *what* is played, but also to *how* it is played. They become essential skills for improvisation, because if you are on stage, it is necessary to listen to the soloist who performs before you so you can respond on the spot to what you heard.

When it comes to listening to the urgings and promptings of the Spirit, we need to develop our ears if we are going to respond in the moment. We can use our Bibles to practice transcribing. It may sound tedious, but try taking a passage of Scripture, preferably a speech by God or an interaction with God, and memorize it. Listen for his tone and become familiar with his cadence. Observe him as he is angry or hurt, and jot down your impressions. Pay attention to his vocabulary, and take note of recurring words as you look for patterns to emerge.

> I discovered a new analytical way of listening to music. The unheard sounds came through, and each melodic line existed in itself, stood out clearly from all the rest, said its piece, and waited patiently for the other voices to speak.
>
> **Ralph Ellison's narrator,**
> ***Invisible Man***

Become a student of his "solos." Then, if and when the moment of Christ incognito arrives, you will be ready to respond, for you will be familiar with his tone and tenor.

These disciplines are the fundamentals to *call-and-response*. Developed ears can enjoy the spontaneous, on-the-spot interplay that happens between two parties. In jazz, listening to the musicians when they find the groove can be a delight to observe. There is nothing like two people who have developed their ears so well that they can take it to this level of play.

This is what I want with God! To become so tuned into his call that we can play together throughout the day like a game of Marco Polo. I want to become so familiar to the Spirit's call that I can respond in tone and in kind to the moment that is presenting itself. I'm hopeful because I think that Jesus had a call-and-response relationship with his Father. And he indicated that we can enjoy a relationship like that as well.

> "Do not believe me unless I do what my Father does."[24]

> "The world must learn that I love the Father and that I do exactly what my Father has commanded me."[25]

> "Do you think I cannot call on my Father, and he will at once put at my disposal more than twelve legions of angels?"[26]

"In that day you will no longer ask me anything. I tell you the truth, my Father will give you whatever you ask in my name."[27]

Developing our ear is not easy. It requires work. It will be worth it though, because *if we have time*, we will be poised to see that every moment of life with Jesus is pregnant with promise—containing the potential of being a one-of-a-kind masterpiece! The essence of jazz is listening—being prepared for the moment, prepared to respond to what the moment offers.

With Christ, no moment is just a moment.

The Dream That Almost Wasn't

When Martin Luther King Jr. stood up before the crowd on a late-August day in 1963, talking about his dream wasn't even on his mind. It wasn't even in his notes. Certainly, he had many wonderful things to say. Poetic lines about withering injustice, cashing a blank check, and letting freedom ring were all in the manuscript that sat in front of him on the podium. But the famous "I Have a Dream" speech is the dream that almost wasn't.

The moment that took place in Washington, D.C., was truly a jazz moment. It was a convergence of preparation, playing off the crowd, improvisation, and listening.

After King was introduced, he began to make his way through his script. As the crowd applauded and shouted, he began to feed off of them. When he said, "We will not be satisfied until justice rolls down like waters, and righteousness like a mighty stream," the crowd began to roar. King began to skip parts of what he had planned—and then it happened.

Prior to King's speech, Mahalia Jackson had sung, "I've Been 'Buked and I've Been Scorned," only to have the crowd demand an encore. So she sang the spiritual, "How I Got Over." After she finished this song, Martin Luther King Jr. was introduced; Mahalia was seated on the stage behind him. What few people know is that she was calling to him. As the great orator was speaking to the nation, she was speaking to him. All he needed to do was respond to her call.

"Tell them about the dream, Martin!"

King continued, already breaking from his script: "Go back to Mississippi, go back to Alabama ..."

Mahalia continued to call: "Tell them about the dream, Martin!"

It was then that it happened—King listened.

Departing from his notes, he began to improvise. He reached back into his memory bank and said, "I still have a dream ..."[28]

What a moment!

singing the blues

*What if so much of what has gone wrong
with America has also produced something that
is right and good, allowing for us to live
and love with soul because we understand
why caged birds sing?*

I'll never forget the young, aspiring jazz singer I saw perform a few summers ago. Several songs into her set, it was clear that her stage presence was poised and her voice pure. Despite her obvious talent, though, something vital was missing. An essential component was absent that made her performance incomplete?

Eventually it dawned on me—it was pain. I couldn't hear any pain in her voice. This was not her fault. She brought to the songs what she had, and pain was not part of her repertoire. For this young lady, it appeared that suffering and disappointment had yet to visit her

in a significant way. Yet, in order for jazz to mature to
a place where it can capture and compel, familiarity
with suffering and pain is necessary.

In 1972, Diana Ross was nominated for five Acad-
emy Awards for her portrayal of Billie Holiday in the
motion picture *Lady Sings the Blues*. It is a sad, autobiographical tale of the legendary jazz singer. Holiday
was born Eleanora Fagan in 1915 and later given the
nickname Lady Day. She is heralded as one of the great
jazz voices of all time. Her voice was unmistakably
unique, though its greatness was not in technical quality; rather, it was in the pain it betrayed.

One generation removed from slavery, Holiday was
the child of a thirteen-year-old mother. She was neglected by her father. Tragically raped as a child and
again as a young woman, she eventually worked in a
Harlem brothel to make ends meet. The pain of di-
vorce, the humiliation of poverty, the hopelessness
of rejection, and the isolation of loneliness all com-
pounded to produce a lady who could sing the blues.

It was Holiday who first sang and recorded the song
"Strange Fruit." I collect every version of this haunting
tale I can find. It's a poem that recollects the "strange
fruit" of Southern trees—that is, lynched men who
had been brutally executed. Only a voice like hers
could sing of such pain so beautifully.

Holiday's quivering voice made painful things

sound attractive. There was a time when Holiday went to her mom for financial help. Her mother rejected her, even though her daughter had come to her aid on many occasions.

Billie Holiday then put pen to paper and wrote "God Bless the Child." In the opening lines she quotes Jesus[1] ("Them that's got shall get, them that's not shall lose") as she laments that religion doesn't always help people treat each other better. So "God bless the child that's got his own." A lyric full of pain, but she made it sound so good.

Billie Holiday died on July 17, 1959, at the age of forty-four due to cirrhosis of the liver. She had seventy cents in the bank.

Red, White, and the Blues

Finding the groove will not be possible if we do not know what to do with pain. The blues set it all in motion. As Ralph Ellison said, "As blues-beset as life may be, the real secret is somehow to make life swing, to survive by staying in the groove."[2]

Life is "blues-beset." The blues, like jazz, are more than music; they are a state of mind. They are "that peculiar feeling that makes you know that there is something seriously wrong with the society, even though you may not possess the intellectual or political power to do anything about it."[3] In Ellison's *Invisible Man*, the narrator was fond of eating a special dish while listening to Louis Armstrong sing, "What Did I Do to Be So Black and Blue." The unnamed narrator says, "Sometimes now I listen to Louis while I have my favorite dessert of vanilla ice cream and sloe gin. I pour the red liquid over the white mound, watching it glisten and the vapor rising as Louis bends that military instrument into a beam of lyrical sound."[4]

That's how Ellison saw America: red, white, and the blues.

Notice the imagery: the *red* of the liquid, the *white* of the ice cream, and Armstrong singing the *blues*. With this as context he then said that all of American life is "jazz shaped."

Red

white

and the blues.

The native soil of this thing called jazz.

Jazz without the blues is like celebrating Jesus' resurrection without recognizing that he was crucified. Most jazz music (or shall I say, good jazz music) pays homage to its blues heritage. Jazz finds its soul in the blues. Jazz music isn't always easy to listen to, and it's rarely popular music. You can try to smooth it out, but at its soul it is not smooth. It was forged in the midst of the pain, grittiness, and rawness of life. Remove the pain, and it becomes soulless. It's hard to make pain smooth, and jazz doesn't attempt to do so. Consequently, a jazz-shaped faith knows how to redeem pain. It recognizes that it is fashioned in circumstances that cause the heart to ache. When we sanitize suffering, we create a soulless faith.

> Jazz speaks for life. The Blues tell the story of life's difficulties, and if you think for a moment, you will realize that they take the hardest realities of life and put them into music, only to come out with some new hope or sense of triumph. This is triumphant music.
> **Martin Luther King Jr., at the Berlin Jazz Festival in 1964**

Why Do Caged Birds Sing?

Have you ever seen a caged bird sing?[5]

In Romania a pastor was imprisoned and tortured without mercy. His captors put him in solitary confinement. Occasionally they would retrieve him, only to cut chunks of flesh from his body. Otherwise he was left to wither without food. It was a brutal existence.

Remarkably, this man survived and would later describe "times when the joy of Christ so overcame him that he would pull himself up and shuffle about the cell in holy dance."[6] When he was set free, he returned home and fasted for a day to commemorate the joy he had found in the midst of his cage.

Have you ever wondered at such a sight?

I'll never forget hearing the story of a girl from El Mozote in northeast El Salvador. This story was told to journalist Mark Danner by the soldiers who had brutalized this girl on a hill called La Cruz—raping her many times during the course of the afternoon:

> Through it all, while the other women of El Mozote had screamed and cried as if they had never had a man, this girl had sung hymns, strange evangelical songs, and she kept right on singing, too, even after they had done what had to be done, and shot her in the chest. She had lain there on La Cruz with the blood flowing from her chest, and had kept on singing—a bit weaker than before, but still singing. And the soldiers, stupefied, had watched and pointed. Then they had grown tired of the game and shot her again, and she sang still, and their wonder began to turn to fear—until finally they had unsheathed their machetes and hacked through her neck, and at last the singing had stopped.[7]

> *They sing because they're happy?*
> *They sing because they're free?*
Beaten, bruised, and brutalized, Fannie Lou Hamer

lay prostrate in her jail cell, unable to stand because of what local law enforcement officials had done to her, all in an attempt to put an end to her voter registration efforts in Mississippi. She could hear them plotting her death. And then she remembered the ancient story of Paul and Silas in prison.[8] She began to sing—and she and her fellow caged birds transformed that dark, damp jail into a cathedral of praise.[9]

His eye is on the sparrow.

It's such an odd sight to see a caged bird sing. All pent-up with no hope of escape. Yet it sings. It blesses, though it is not blessed. Ornithology is the study of birds. Those involved in this endeavor have surmised that the reason the caged bird sings is the same reason uncaged birds sing; they sing for love. In the wild, the song of the bird is for the purpose of attracting a mate. That desire cannot be taken away by mere confinement.

And I know he watches me.

Jesus sang.

In the upper room before they left for the place known as the "olive press," he and the disciples sang a hymn.[10] Less than twenty-four hours later, Jesus hung on the cross, and in the midst of excruciating pain he sang again: " '*Eloi, Eloi, lama sabachthani?*' —which means, 'My God, my God, why have you forsaken me?' "[11]

I don't think Jesus calmly quoted this question. I

think he was singing. After all, the words originate from an ancient Hebrew song about his crucifixion — written and set to music centuries before he hung on the cross.

Jesus sang.

　　　For love.

That's why caged birds sing.

　　　He sang because we can now be happy.

　　He sang because we are now free.

Jesus sang the blues!

Tragicomic Hope

Musically speaking, the blues are simple. They most often consist of a twelve-bar sequence, a chorus, that is repeated over and over with infinite variations. Its power is not in its complexity but in the story it tells.

Existentially speaking, the blues are a way of dealing with suffering. They are therapy. The blues are a narrative wrought out of the deep feelings that accompany life in a world that isn't as it should be. To sing the blues is to latch on to a tragedy in such a way that we embrace it for all its worth. It is to become intimately familiar with the details of our suffering. This is the most difficult part of composing a jazz-shaped faith. It requires that we become intimately familiar with our pain and the pain of the world. As Ralph Ellison noted, "The blues is an impulse to keep the painful details and episodes of a brutal experience alive in one's aching consciousness, to finger its jagged grain, and to transcend it, not by the consolation of philosophy but by squeezing from it a near-tragic, near-comic lyricism."[12]

"Near-tragic, near-comic": *Tragicomic hope*.[13] The blues make a comedy out of tragedy. Rooted in the stuff of life, the blues seek to find meaning in sorrow. A blues artist sings about that which has gone wrong and will keep singing until it turns upside down, until the smile appears. Through its repetition, it seeks to work out the pain until the pain gives way to a joke.

The Bible is familiar with the blues. Just consider the book of Job. God makes a wager with the accuser, the Devil, about his faithful servant Job, and literally all hell breaks loose in Job's life. As you work your way through the forty-two chapters of speeches given by Job, his friends, and ultimately God, you find yourself smiling on a few occasions in spite of the tragedy.

Paul said that he was "not ashamed of the gospel."[14] At first, it sounds so admirable. But then the question creeps to mind, "What's to be ashamed of anyway?" Who would be ashamed of good news unless there was something about it that was a little odd? And indeed, the gospel is a cosmic comedic tragedy—a tragicomic hope.

Paul wrote, "We preach Christ crucified: a stumbling block to Jews and foolishness to Gentiles."[15] I wish I could preach the gospel like Paul. I am too good at making it sound attractive. I mean, have you ever thought about those two words together—*Christ crucified*. How can that be? Christ (the long-awaited, anointed Messiah of God) crucified (tortured, disgraced, subjected to suffering—even though he did nothing wrong). No wonder Paul's audience had a hard time with his message. Jews needed rescuing from the Romans— and Christ died at the hands of their imperialistic rulers. The Romans respected power—and crushed God with their might. I wish I could get comfortable with making the gospel as incongruous as it really is. The gospel is a great reversal. Up is down. Right is left. Death is life. Christ crucified!

> Jazz is music made by and for people who have chosen to feel good in spite of conditions.
>
> **Johnny Griffin,**
> **tenor saxophonist**

Jesus knew how to make the good news sound absurd.

Do you remember when Jesus asked his disciples if his teaching offended them, and many of them turned back and no longer followed him?[16] It was because of tragicomic hope.

What led to their desertion? Jesus fed the five thousand and then snuck away in the middle of the night. When the crowd found him again, he decided to explain that there was another kind of bread they should want: "For the bread of God is he who comes down from heaven.... I am the bread of life."[17] Shortly after that statement, the crowd began to grumble. Now, instead of taking the time to explain the metaphor, Jesus decides to take it to the absurd: "This bread is my flesh, which I will give for the life of the world."[18]

Couldn't he have stopped to explain the connection with the manna in the desert and that his death on the cross was going to be like that? Couldn't he have made a nice little connection to the Lord's Supper for them? No, not Jesus. For him, the good news has to have an edge to it. It has to have a twist. The good news needed to sound like bad news—with a smile.

> "I tell you the truth, unless you eat the flesh of the Son of Man and drink his blood, you have no life in you. Whoever eats my flesh and drinks my blood has eternal life, and I will raise him up at the last day. For my flesh is real food and my blood is real drink. Whoever eats my flesh and drinks my blood remains in me, and I in him."[19]

Now that's absurd gospel, according to Jesus:

Bite me!

The gospel is for those whose lives have reached

tragicomic proportions. When I read Paul's description of his life in Romans 7, I grin because it sounds like the tragedy of my life too: "I do not understand what I do. For what I want to do I do not do, but what I hate I do.... What a wretched man I am! Who will rescue me from this body of death?"[20]

There is something about seeing how utterly absurd it is to sin in light of such a magnificent God. It brings us to a place of comedic tragedy. God calls me to the Christian life but then says I can't live it. My only choice is to die and let Christ live it in me. When we let that truth sink in, then—and only then—are we ready to receive the gospel in its totality: "Christ in you, the hope of glory."[21]

Mo' Better Blues*

There are a lot of reasons to stay clear of sin. Most compelling to me is that it disrupts the natural flow of the Holy Spirit in our lives. God in his mercy is willing to work in and through sinful vessels; the problem is that sinful vessels rarely allow him to do so. When we are focused on sin or sinning, we are in a place where it becomes difficult to receive God's grace. This is because, when we're in such a place, we can't believe

---

* With acknowledgments to Spike Lee.

that God would really desire to use us. Confession and repentance are important so that we can face the disturbances—those things that limit our ability to walk in grace—that we allow into our lives.

But it must be more than that. Sin isn't the only thing that causes us to lose the groove. I once heard it said that there is no difference between the person focused on sinning and the person focused on not sinning—neither is focused on Jesus![22]

When you think about it, it really makes absolutely no sense why we choose the temporary insanity of sin. In light of who Jesus is, why would we ever take our eyes off of him? Yet we do! And when we do, our only option to deal with the pain is to sing the blues until the tragedy we have created gives way to hope.

Confession is a form of the blues.

King David was guilty of adultery and murder.[23] After the prophet Nathan confronted him about his sin,[24] David lamented in song—which we know of as Psalm 51. David's words are a classic blues saga, full of begging, pleading, honesty, and acknowledgment. The first twelve verses are an agonizing journey of recognizing the reality of stepping outside of the bounds of God's love. It even possesses tragicomic hope. You almost laugh halfway through when David sings to God, "Then I will teach transgressors your ways, and sinners will turn back to you." What?! If God has mercy and

will grant the audacious requests of cleansing and res-
toration, then David has a deal for God: he will teach
sinners the ways of God.

It would be funny except for the fact that you and
I have done the same thing. Haven't we?

We've looked at the bad decisions in our lives and
then asserted to God, "You could really use this stuff!"
That's the hope in the tragedy of confession. That we
serve a God who actually can — and does — redeem
everything, even our sin. The paradox of confession
is that we turn our backs on God. Doing so, in turn,
drives us to our knees and into his presence, and there
we experience the sweetness of his grace on the heels
of our sin.

Samson was another biblical character who knew
the mo' better blues.

Chosen from birth and set apart for God, this
strong man never seemed to recognize how special his
situation was. Perhaps he took it for granted or thought
everyone had similar experiences. Through the years,
he continually compromised the promise of God on
his life. And then came the ultimate mistake: he revealed the secret of his power to the infamous betrayer,
Delilah.

The tragedy: gouged-out eyes, shackled and in
prison, head shaved.

The comedy: little stubbles of hair were returning.

The hope: he accomplished more in his death than in his life.[25]

If we are to possess a jazz-shaped faith, then we can't run from the pain we have caused by our sin. We must embrace its jagged edges, knowing that in Christ and in the economy of his kingdom, not one drop of our worst moments need be wasted.

> God has wrought many things out of oppression. He has endowed his creatures with the capacity to create—and from this capacity has flowed the sweet songs of sorrow and joy that have allowed man to cope with his environment and many different situations.
>
> **Martin Luther King Jr., at the Berlin Jazz Festival in 1964**

Blues People*

Buddy Bolden was a little crazy.

He is also recognized by many jazz historians as the "father of jazz." Check out this description:

He played so forcefully that his trumpet could be heard all over New Orleans. Given the fact that

---

* Acknowledgments to LeRoi Jones (Amiri Baraka), who wrote a classic work by the same title.

there is little documentation of the man himself, much less his music, this was thought to be just another Crescent City Myth. But was it? New Orleans, after all, lies below sea level, and it has acoustical properties like those of an echo chamber. Add to that the lack of cars and similar distractions at that time, and maybe the stories about Bolden sticking his cornet out of the club to alert the town to his presence really are true.[26]

Even so, New Orleans, the Big Easy, was anything but easy for Buddy Bolden. This jazz genius and early explorer of improvisation was committed to an insane asylum in 1906.

Sometimes I wonder if God can be known outside of subpar conditions, caves, and a little bit of insanity. It seems to me that Jesus is bending his ear, listening for those who cry to him out of the echo chambers, the pain, and the craziness of life. That's why he took his disciples out on the water and into the wind and waves—and calmed the storm around them.[27] There was a man who lived in the caves, crying out—he was singing the blues. Jesus heard him, and Jesus calmed the storm that raged in

> As a form, the blues is an autobiographical chronicle of personal catastrophe expressed lyrically.
>
> **Ralph Ellison, author and jazz expert**

this man's soul.[28] In the same way that jazz won't let us forget the blues, Jesus' message won't let us forget the least of these—the blues people. The gospel must connect with the poor and the poor in spirit, the miserable and the marginalized, in order for it to be the gospel. When Jesus spoke of the gospel, he did so in terms of a kingdom for blues people (and beyond).[29]

The good news that Christ proclaimed and demonstrated was connected to a larger, more encompassing vision that included forgiveness of sins yet was so much bigger. The kingdom is about the shalom—the peace, wholeness, well-being—and overarching influence of God in every area of life. As Mark said, the gospel is big enough to include "all creation."[30] It is an alternative reality that speaks to every area of life, including the painful elements. As a matter of fact, you know it's the true gospel when it is applied to the pain and in the impoverished areas of our lives and society. The gospel is the good news that Jubilee—liberation, release—has arrived.

[Jesus] went to Nazareth, where he had been brought up, and on the Sabbath day he went into the synagogue, as was his custom. And he stood up to read. The scroll of the prophet Isaiah was handed to him. Unrolling it, he found the place where it is written:

"The Spirit of the Lord is on me,
   because he has anointed me
   to preach good news to the poor.
He has sent me to proclaim freedom for the
   prisoners
   and recovery of sight for the blind,
to release the oppressed,
   to proclaim the year of the Lord's favor."

Then he rolled up the scroll, gave it back to the attendant and sat down. The eyes of everyone in the synagogue were fastened on him, and he began by saying to them, "Today this Scripture is fulfilled in your hearing."[31]

Speaking of God's concern for the least of these, Anglican churchman Chris Sugden wrote, "What the good news means to them is to define what it is to mean to all."[32] Or let me say it this way, if our gospel doesn't have the blues in it and if it's not applicable to blues people, then it's not the gospel.

Jesus says that the gospel is about how the poor are really rich and the prisoner (the caged bird) is truly free. It is about how the blind can see because we walk by faith and not by sight. It is good news to the poor, the down-and-out, the disenfranchised, those deemed unimportant, the unborn, and the oppressed, because God identifies with and has become one of them.[33]

Jesus showed us that he was good news, even to

a caged bird like John the Baptist. When John was in prison, he sent some of his disciples to Jesus to confirm that he was the Messiah. We can understand why. John gave his life to prepare the way for Jesus, and now

> I tell you the truth, whatever you did for one of the least of these brothers of mine, you did for me.
>
> **Jesus Christ**

he was in prison singing the blues. Had he done something wrong? Was Jesus really the one for whom they had been waiting?

Jesus' response was that the presence of pain and suffering was wholly compatible with the coming of the kingdom of God. Victory was not going to be experienced as release from prison for John. As a matter of fact, John had a front-row seat to this new reality right where he was. Jesus said:

> "Go back and report to John what you hear and see: The blind receive sight, the lame walk, those who have leprosy are cured, the deaf hear, the dead are raised, and the good news is preached to the poor. Blessed is the man who does not fall away on account of me."[34]

The gospel we live must be for blues people. A jazz-shaped faith is familiar with life on the bottom. It is comfortable with the poor and the poor in spirit, the marginalized and the miserable—for they are Jesus.

What Color Is Jesus?

James Cone said, "Jesus is black."[35]

This statement made many people uncomfortable. After all, what does it matter? Assertions like this can only cause arguments, and in the end, what difference would it make?

Even if we decide that the question "What color is Jesus?" has merit, the answer is a slam dunk, right? In the flesh he was a typical Middle Eastern man with commensurate features.

James Cone knew this, and yet he still emphatically said that Jesus is black. The reason he made such a statement is often misunderstood because he was improvising. Most people fail to recognize the song.

Notice the verb tense that Cone used. He didn't say Jesus *was* black. No, he said Jesus *is* black. It isn't a statement about Jesus' literal skin tone but rather an attempt to play an old song in a new way. If we are going to experience ancient truths as reality today, we must be willing to take the risk of improvisation. Sometimes, of course, we will fall flat, and that is why we need the safety of our ensemble. With the ensemble, the risk is worth it, because we may happen upon something that will allow for the gospel to be good news in ways we did not foresee.

James Cone made this point when he wrote the following in 1975:

> If twentieth-century Christians are to speak the truth for the sociohistorical situation, they cannot merely repeat the story of what Jesus did and said in Palestine, as if it were self-interpreting for us today. Truth is more than the retelling of the biblical story. Truth is the divine happening that invades our contemporary situation, revealing the meaning of the past for the present so that we are made new creatures for the future.[36]

Seeking God in the moment is a never-ending pursuit for faith inspired by jazz. We live for that space in time when our hunger for God and his eternal song and our questions, joys, and pains converge with Jesus —"the divine happening that invades our contemporary situation" Cone asserts we must know Jesus as he *was*, as he *is, and* also as he *will be*.[37]

So what color is Jesus? Well, we know what color he *was* (a Middle Eastern man with all the telltale characteristics). We can only imagine what color he *will be* when we see him face-to-face (with eyes like fire and feet like bronze).[38] But what color will he be to you and me today?

What do you say? What color *is* Jesus?

First of all, in order to answer this question, we

need to make sure we're all playing the same song. Listen to the words of our Composer:

> "For I was hungry and you gave me something to eat, I was thirsty and you gave me something to drink, I was a stranger and you invited me in, I needed clothes and you clothed me, I was sick and you looked after me, I was in prison and you came to visit me....
>
> "I tell you the truth, whatever you did for one of the least of these brothers of mine, you did for me."[39]

When James Cone said, "Jesus is black," he was playing off of these words of Jesus. He was seeking to make Jesus' words about "the least of these" relevant to the time and place in which he found himself in history. This is a must if we want to truly experience Jesus today, for he tells us where to find him.

"Whatever you have done for one of the least of these brothers of mine, you did for me."

Those words are so familiar that we often miss their not-so-subtle hint. Do you want to experience the real presence of Jesus? Find the least of these in your context, and you will find the hangout of Jesus!

James Cone was writing just a few generations after the end of slavery. Up until that point, African-Americans had only been able to vote for two of the

United States' thirty-eight presidents. With the melody of the least of these playing through his head, Cone asked who the least of these would be in America. To answer this question would lead to a profound encounter with Jesus Christ. Then, as now, many answers would arise: the mentally ill in an asylum, the Native Americans on a reservation, and the abject poor of Appalachia, to name just a few. Improvising, Cone decided to ask the question in terms of skin color. Saying "Jesus is black" in 1975 was to recognize that current reality for a specific group of people — those who were only three generations removed from four hundred years of slavery and in the midst of another hundred years of striving for equality. That is how James Cone syncopated the song of the least of these in 1975. That was then. This is now.

The song of Jesus is eternal, though our circumstances, setting, and questions change. Jazz is all about moments that may or may not be reproduced. It is about leaving room for people to take solos that we may or may not like. Jazz is about playing the same song a new way each time because of the convergence of the audience, the band, and any number of other factors with the hope of hearing things in a new way. A jazz-shaped faith is free to experiment because of the safety of the eternal word of God and the community of Jesus Christ with whom we will spend eternity.

Cone realized that the version of the song he was playing would last only for a moment that would pass away. He in no way thought that Jesus was and always would be black. He admitted the temporality of his interpretation. Cone did not think that what he said was true for the distant future or for every context.[40]

So what do you say? What color is Jesus? Black? Black and blue? I think he's *Kind of Blue* ...

so what

Jesus was a master jazz theologian.
Carl Ellis

When I first bought *Kind of Blue*, I didn't realize how special it was. I was just trying to build my jazz music collection, and I'd heard that Miles Davis was someone to be familiar with. It became one of my favorite albums, and I quickly wore out the cassette tape. At the time I couldn't have explained why the songs were so compelling. All I knew is that I couldn't stop listening. Now that I know the story, it all makes sense.

Kind of Blue was recorded by Miles Davis in 1959, and it's one of the best-selling jazz albums ever. It was named one of the ten best albums in *any* category during end-of-the-century polls. *Kind of Blue* is the only jazz album to achieve double platinum status, and it continues to sell strong today. With trumpet in hand,

Miles called together an ensemble comprised of tenor saxophonist John Coltrane, alto saxophonist Cannonball Adderley, bassist Paul Chambers, and drummer Jimmy Cobb. This group of practiced musicians combined to produce what some have called the most influential jazz album of all time. Many believe that jazz history divides into two segments—"before *Kind of Blue* and after *Kind of Blue*."[1]

"So What" is the subtle yet unforgettable first song on *Kind of Blue*. On the back cover of the album, there isn't a question mark after the title "So What." This wasn't a typographical error. It looks like it should be a query, but it's not. "So What" is a declaration. Eric Nisenson observes, "Kind of Blue was created ... because the most important jazzmen in the modern scene desperately wanted to change the way they played their music. This need was not purely musical; it had more than a little to do with the changes then going on in American society."[2]

"So What" was a statement: *The old is gone, the new has come!*[3]

Kind of Blue marked the end of an era for jazz music and the beginning of something fresh. It pre-called what was about to happen in American society. To grasp this, we need to remember what life in America was like in the years leading up to 1959. The war was over, the invention of suburbia was underway, and, for most, the pursuit of the American Dream was back on track.

Yet in the African-American community, the 1950s were a decade of tension. After ninety years of blacks' not being slaves and yet not being citizens either, something had to give. The dehumanization of separate water fountains, segregated schools, lynchings in the South, massive nihilism in the urban North, and absence of voting rights gave rise to discontent. As Fannie Lou Hamer would say, sometimes you're just "sick and tired of being sick and tired."[4]

At the same time, jazz music had an inferiority complex. It was always compared to classical music and never felt as legitimate as its European counterpart. Jazz music pre-1959 too often sought to conform to classical standards, complete with big bands modeled after orchestras. Not satisfied with this, many jazz musicians were experimenting with new ways of playing in jazz, as they pondered the question, "What if classical music was 'a' standard but not 'the' standard?"

Before 1959, which is pre–*Kind of Blue*, conformity was the way of seeking acceptance into the melting pot of the American Dream. This was seen as the key to success for many African-Americans in general and jazz musicians in particular. Larger society thought that jazz music was simply the product of an innate sense for rhythm of African-Americans and that it was nowhere near as sophisticated as classical music. Black musicians sought to counteract this perception by increasing the complexity of their music in an attempt to demonstrate that it was a music of intelligence. All of this created a visceral uneasiness. With black soldiers fighting a war against hate and fascism in Europe, they found it difficult to return to a country still having to prove themselves.[5]

Around the time of the recording and release of *Kind of Blue*, Miles Davis used to do something that some found offensive: he would play with his back to the audience. Unable to use the same restrooms or entrances as his white patrons, Miles wanted to make a statement as he stood on stage. Some saw this as an act of arrogance. Others saw it and began to hope. After all, if a mere musician would dare turn his back in protest to society, then what else was possible— common drinking fountains, same schools, voting rights, no more lynchings?

There was another reason why he played with his back to his listeners. Miles once said that by turning and facing the band, he could listen better, read their cues, and ultimately produce a better musical experience for the audience. In spite of his disdain for a society that contained so much blatant inequality, he sought to give a gift.

Musically, Miles Davis decided to blaze a new trail

with a new set of standards. After seeing an African dance troupe and listening with amazement to the beats of the drummers, he set aside European chord progressions as the best way to play jazz and went with what is called a modal approach, based on scales. And in a two-day recording session, *Kind of Blue* emerged. It became "a watershed in the history of jazz, a signpost pointing to the tumultuous changes that would dominate this music and society itself in the decade ahead."[6]

Indeed, something was afoot. In 1954, racial segregation of schools was ruled unconstitutional. In 1955, Rosa Parks decided to stay seated on a city bus. In 1959, Miles Davis recorded *Kind of Blue*. Four years later, Martin Luther King Jr. called America to live out the true meaning of our creed.

Jazz anticipates *and* participates as it senses the shift of the wind. It listens.

If you decide to adopt a jazz-shaped faith, you will become a statement. No longer will you be satisfied with a series of static propositions or the status quo. Rather, you will begin to sense current realities, anticipating the Spirit of God as the old passes and the new arrives.

Listen to IT. Respond to IT. Live IT.

What is IT? IT is not a question; IT is a statement. Jesus and his gospel was and is a proclamation. IT is the radical, life-altering, world-shaking assertion that the kingdom of God has arrived.[7] The good news that Jesus announced with his lips, demonstrated with his life, sealed on the cross, and inaugurated with his resurrection is nothing short of the reality that the way and the will of God is here for all people.

Jesus is kind of blue, for with every word and deed he proclaimed IT: *the old is gone, the new has come.*

So What Is the Statement?

A statement needs to be made in the midst of the consumeristic, power-laden, individualized culture in which we swim. We know it. But what is the statement that a jazz-shaped faith will make? Some say *revival*. In general, I believe America needs revival, but I'm not sure that's what the church needs. After all, revival assumes something is dead. I don't think the church is dead, just largely ineffective. *Repentance* is another alternative. Jesus called believer and unbeliever alike to "repent, for the kingdom of heaven is near."[8] To repent simply means to turn from one way of life to another, but this raises the obvious question, "What are we turning to?" *Reformation* and *renewal* are also good statements. It's never a bad thing to return to the basics and remind ourselves who we are and what we are to be about. What about *revolution*? It's close; however,

Jesus started the revolution two thousand years ago, and it's continued ever since. I don't think the church needs a revolution more than we need to join the one already in progress.

There is nothing wrong with any of these statements per se, but I think a jazz-shaped faith points us in a different direction, toward something more foundational to jazz itself: *renaissance*. Christianity in America needs to experience a renaissance.

Harlem, That Is ...

Renaissance is a beautiful word which simply means "rebirth."

We are all renaissance people. The question is, "Which one?"

Most of us are familiar with the classical renaissance that is usually called "The Renaissance" (more accurately, "The Italian or European Renaissance"), which took place during the late 1300s to 1600s. It was a time when classical thought was applied to reason, rhetoric, art, science, literature, poetry, architecture, and music.

America also had a renaissance. Ours was a jazz-shaped rebirth of culture. It took place in Harlem during the 1920s to 1940s and then spread across the country. The Harlem Renaissance was a time in which jazz flourished in all areas of our culture. It permeated the way people wrote, spoke, dressed, and even played sports. Take basketball, for example. Before the Harlem Renaissance, it was a game of dribbling, passing, and layups. Then jazz, with the concepts of syncopation, improvisation, and call-and-response transformed the game forever. Hence, the Harlem Globetrotters!

The Harlem Renaissance was the jazz age. It was the time when Langston Hughes asked about what happens when a dream is deferred—and Ralph Ellison responded. It was the place where Duke Ellington reigned as king of swing and Bonhoeffer visited. Harlem was where Billie Holiday honed her skills and sang about "strange fruit." It is what provided the foundation for the collaborations of Miles Davis and John Coltrane.

So which renaissance is ours? Thankfully we don't have to choose. The Italian Renaissance gave us Leonardo da Vinci, Machiavelli, Michelangelo, Copernicus, and Descartes. The Harlem Renaissance gave us Ralph Ellison, James Baldwin, Zora Neal Hurston, W. E. B. Du Bois, and Langston Hughes. When it comes to our faith, think of it this way: *One renaissance gave us a worldview, and the other gave us a way of viewing the world.*

As Christians, it is vital to have a biblical worldview. That is, right thinking sustains right living. We can't know what Jesus would do if we don't know what Jesus did. To that end, the *Italian* Renaissance ultimately produced *Martin Luther.* He was a German monk and scholar so surrendered to Jesus, the church, and the Scriptures that he devoted his life to actually knowing what the Bible says and paving a way for others to see it for themselves.

The Harlem Renaissance gave us a Martin Luther as well — Martin Luther King Jr. He pointed us to a way of viewing the world as he stood on the accomplishments of his predecessor and namesake. To see the world as God does — this caused him to take the church into the streets, not to ask a question, but to make a statement.

We don't have to choose between these two renaissances, but — unfortunately — I think we have. That's why I wrote this book. So much of American Christianity is influenced by the Italian Renaissance. That's great, but all the while we unnecessarily neglect the benefits of the renaissance that took place here on our own soil. If we could end this neglect and also embrace the Harlem Renaissance as *our* renaissance, then — like our nation's culture in the middle of the last century — the American church could experience a jazz age. A rebirth that gives individuals in the church a chance to find their unique voices in ensemble community, appreciating pain and the gift of creative tension.

What a Wonderful World

Louis Armstrong's career started before the jazz age and survived after it. He was a contemporary of Miles Davis and served as a complement to him.

If Louis Armstrong didn't invent the solo, he at least perfected it. Before Louis, jazz was primarily about the group. Then this trumpeter from New Orleans began playing in a way that you couldn't help but notice him within the group. Consequently, breaks were added to highlight his individual talents. Now it's hard for us to imagine jazz without solos, but there was a time when solos weren't commonplace. Louis Armstrong was a jazz ambassador, and he took its message all over the world.

> Louis Armstrong is quite simply the most important person in American music. He is to twentieth-century music (I did not say jazz) what Einstein is to physics, Freud is to psychiatry, and the Wright Brothers are to travel.
>
> **Ken Burns, documentary filmmaker**

There was something special about Louis. Some say it was his improvisational skills on the trumpet, and others point to his vocals—both of which were truly unique and amazing. What strikes me about Louis was his way of viewing the world. At a time when race relations were far from good, he was able to step into even the most segregated of settings and make people feel welcome. He viewed the world differently. Remember his song, "What a Wonderful World"? Armstrong's 1970 recording of this song included this spoken introduction:

> Some of you young folks been saying to me, "Hey, Pops, what you mean 'What a wonderful world'? How about all them wars all over the place? You call them wonderful? And how about hunger and pollution? That ain't so wonderful either." Well how about listening to old Pops for a minute. Seems to me, it ain't the world that's so bad but what we're doin' to it. And all I'm saying is, see, what a wonderful world it would be if only we'd give it a chance. Love, baby, love. That's the secret, yeah.[9]

A worldview and a way of viewing the world. Say it with me:

> Oh, yeaaaahhhh!

A Jazz Theologian

I deeply desire to be a part of a generation of people who understand what IT is — a generation of jazz theologians. I am not "the" jazz theologian; I am simply "a" jazz theologian. I am hoping to be one of many who seek to understand the way of Jesus in postmovement America. We have yet to fully own what it means to live out the ideals of the "beloved community" for which those in the Civil Rights Movement sacrificed. The night before Martin Luther King Jr. was assassinated, he said he had been to the mountaintop and seen the Promised Land. I believe we are standing on the banks of the Jordan, and that which he saw, we can enter.

> Can you see IT?
> taste IT?
> smell IT?
> the land flowing with milk
> and honey — the kingdom of God
> in our own place and time

If you answered "yes" to any of these questions, then you might be a jazz theologian too. Seek *syncopation*. Hear that which is so often missed, and accent the offbeat until IT begins to swing. Find the groove, and set the Spirit of God free to *improvise* in you and through you. Hone your skills, and begin to *call* and see if there are others who will answer in *response*.

Recognize that jazz exists only because America exists and that it is a unique medium by which to translate the gospel. Embrace the mystery and tension of your faith, and let it lead you deep into a relationship with the

> Jazz is played from the heart. You can even live by it.
>
> **Louis Armstrong, jazz trumpeter and singer**

most creative being in the universe and the third-way thinking of Jesus. *Have time* to develop your ear so that you can hear those around you and live in concert with them. Get to *the woodshed* and practice! Practice the ways of Jesus so that others can confidently count on you when you take the stage. Dig deep into God's word, not for the purpose of regurgitation, but so you can join in with the melody of the Spirit's eternal song and add your own voice to that of the ancients. And when pain visits, don't forget to finger its jagged edges—*sing the blues*—until those around you have no choice but to smile in recognition of the living cruci-fied Christ in your life!

A jazz theologian is simply someone who realizes that jazz is more than music and that IT is the "more" that will make the statement. Music happens to be the realm in which most of us recognize jazz, but I think Ralph Ellison got it right when he said that all of American life is "jazz-shaped." Jazz is a way of thinking and a way of viewing the world. It is about freedom within community. It is a culture, a set of values and norms by which we can experience life in general and faith in particular. It is about how we know things. Jazz knowing is a knowledge born out of experience. It is a knowledge based on taking the proposition and living it.

A jazz theologian is simply someone who realizes that theology (the study of God) is only relevant when it actually leads us to interact with the God who has stooped and revealed himself to his creation. It is not dry systems that are codified in books. Theology is the result of a person who presses in to the Almighty with an intense passion to know God in all of his paradox and mystery. Theology comes alive as we follow Jesus, seeking to know the truth of God as we walk with him—living the truth.

A jazz theologian is simply someone who wants God to use him or her in the same way he used ordinary people just like them in the past. I want to be a jazz theologian because my heart aches to be part of a church so surrendered to God that we experience his power in the same way the early church did in the first century. I want to be like those early Christians who stepped into a world in which women were owned, children were cheap labor, poverty was the lot of the majority, slavery was assumed, the disabled were discarded, religion was incarcerating, and the government was oppressive. Yet by the time they spilled their blood on the streets of Rome, they had turned their world upside down.[10] They introduced love and covenant into marriage, providing a safe haven for women and children. There were no needy people among them, because those who had much ensured that none had too little.[11] Though the institution of slavery remained, it became obsolete, as slave and owner worshiped the one true Master together. Those with disabilities were honored, for they had been counted worthy to suffer like Jesus. Believers permeated the government, even into Caesar's household.[12] And new names were written daily in the book of life.

A jazz theologian is someone who makes a statement — back turned to the world and yet still seeking to be a blessing. A jazz theologian is someone who knows deeply what IT is ...

and says IT

lives IT

hears IT

loves IT enough to find IT

Have you found your groove? Let the composed life begin ...

acknowledgments

Every Lent I submit my dreams to God.

As I prepare to celebrate the reality that Jesus conquered death, I take my dreams to God and allow them to die—both the ones I am living and those yet unrealized. I place them in the tomb with Jesus on Good Friday. It's a ritual that focuses me on Jesus rather than on what I want him to do for me.

I remember when I was single and wanting to be married. I couldn't figure out why the Lord wasn't providing for me. On Good Friday of 1993, I placed my dream of being married in the tomb and prayed, "Lord, you rose on the third day; bring back to life only the dreams that you desire to live." Later that year I met Barbara—thanks be to God!

The dreams that are not resurrected remain in the tomb, waiting to see when or if God will give them life. Two years ago, Jesus surprised me by breathing life into a dead dream—to be a writer.

Many times I've been told that I should write a book. The idea has always been appealing, but reservations have abounded. First, there was the question of motivation. Why write a book? Is it just to say, I wrote a book? Then there was a little nagging fact—Oh yeah, I'm not a writer! That was one of my largest barriers. The fear of trying to do something that isn't a competency was less than appealing. Eventually, I remembered people like Phillis Wheatley and Frederick Douglass—former slaves with nowhere near the education or opportunity I've been afforded. If they could write a book, so could I. Finally, there was the practical question of what I would write about. As with sermons, I wanted a sense of calling and anointing. I needed to sense that God was giving me a message. It was a few years ago, after celebrating Easter services, that I felt the Spirit breathing life into this old dream of mine—I am humbled and grateful.

To the One who has always been there, my song, my caller, my friend, and my Lord—you were present from the moment I was conceived. Have thine own way, Lord. Have thine own way!

To my wife Barbara—you are my heart and soul. A lifetime is not enough to show you how much I am privileged to serve you.

To my children:

  Selah: Shine, dance—let his glory
    be your beauty.
  Kia: God chose you; always choose God.
  Gabriel: Let God be your strength.
  James: Let God's joy keep you on your knees.
  Mihret: Always be an ambassador
    for the mercy of God.
  Temesgen: Go for broke, for God is with you.

To my family:

  Mom: You gave me life. I am forever indebted
    to you for your sacrifice.
  Dad: You gave me two great names, Robert and
    Gelinas. Thank you for the gift of identity.
  Bro's: Dennis and Roland—Did you hear that?
    Swish!
  Bra's: Chris, Tina, Katrina, Sierra—I love you.

To Colorado Community Church—I would be a part of you even if I wasn't your pastor. Your love for God, passion for worship, and willingness to wash the feet of our city make you an indispensable part of the kingdom of God. Staff and board of directors—I am honored to serve our King alongside you.

To all of you who have encouraged me to write and supported me during this journey—Elisa Morgan,

Craig Williford, Scott Dewey, Jeff Johnsen, Chris and Sarah Padbury, Pete Gall, Dave Noller, Debbie and Joe Rillos—heartfelt thanks.

To Stace Tafoya—what can I say!

To Carl Ellis—your writings are brilliant and God inspired. Our Lord has shown you what is to be, the Promised Land. You have sounded the trumpet—let the Joshua Generation rise up!

To Wolgemuth and Associates—Robert, Andrew, and Erik—I believe our partnership is God ordained, and I couldn't have done this without you.

Soli Deo Gloria!

notes

Chapter 1: Setting the Stage

1. Daniel Taylor, *The Myth of Certainty: Trusting God, Asking Questions, Taking Risks* (Grand Rapids: Zondervan, 1992), 29.
2. Charles Marsh, *The Beloved Community: How Faith Shapes Social Justice, from the Civil Rights Movement to Today* (New York: Basic Books, 2005), 215.
3. For a readable yet scholarly treatment of the subject, just read the work of Philip Jenkins (*The Next Christendom: The Coming of Global Christianity* [New York: Oxford Univ. Press, 2002]), in which he explores the implications of the shift of the epicenter of Christianity in the world. By the year 2050, one out of five Christians will live in the southern hemisphere and be non-Latino and nonwhite.
4. Acts 17.

Chapter 2: More Than Music

1. This is only one among many theories on the derivation of jazz.
2. Whitney Balliett, *The Sound of Surprise* (New York: E. P. Dutton, 1959).

3. Ray Charles, *Genius + Soul = Jazz* album (Impulse! 1961).

4. Cited in Nat Hentoff, "Jazz Is Coming Home to Harlem," *Wall Street Journal*, March 18, 2004, *www.jazzmuseuminharlem.org/ wsj_31804.html*.

5. Ralph Ellison, *Living with Music: Ralph Ellison's Jazz Writings* (New York: Modern Library, 2002), xi, xiii.

6. *Jazz: A Film by Ken Burns* (ten episodes; PBS Home Video, 2001). If you haven't seen this, it is worth the investment to purchase it or the trip to check it out of your local library.

7. Geoffrey C. Ward and Ken Burns, *Jazz: A History of America's Music* (New York: Knopf, 2000), vii.

8. Brad R. Braxton, *No Longer Slaves: Galatians and African American Experience* (Collegeville, Minn.: Liturgical Press, 2002), 19.

9. Genesis 50:20.

Chapter 3: Key Notes

1. Luke 8:40–48.

2. David Hajdu, "Wynton's Blues," *The Atlantic*, March 2003, *www.theatlantic.com/doc/200303/hajdu*.

3. Genesis 18; Exodus 32; Jonah 1.

4. Luke 12:11–12.

5. "Harlem (2)," from *The Collective Poems of Langston Hughes* by Langston Hughes, edited by Arnold Rampersad, with David Roessel, assoc. ed. Copyright © 1994 by The Estate of Langston Hughes. Used by permission of Alfred A. Knopf, a division of Random House, Inc.

Chapter 4: Creative Tension

1. John 11:1–44.

2. Genesis 1.

3. C. S. Lewis, *The Magician's Nephew* (New York: Harper-Collins, 1955), 116–26.

4. Genesis 1; John 1; Colossians 1:16–17.
5. Psalm 139:13.
6. Ephesians 2:10.
7. Exodus 31:1–5. See also Exodus 35:30–35.
8. Psalm 46:10.
9. John 3:3.
10. John 4:10–14; Luke 23:43; Matthew 12:38–42.
11. James Lucas, *Knowing the Unknowable God* (Colorado Springs: WaterBrook, 2003), 4–5.
12. Ibid., 20.
13. John 8:1–11.
14. John 14:6.
15. Cited in Annie Dillard, *The Writing Life* (New York: Harper & Row, 1989), 12.
16. Proverbs 25:2.
17. Colossians 1:25–27.
18. Matthew 11:25.
19. Matthew 13:44.
20. Revelation 2:4.
21. John 13:1–17.
22. Galatians 5:6.
23. John Coltrane, *A Love Supreme* (Impulse! 1965), liner notes.
24. Romans 7:7–23.
25. Matthew 26:31–35, 69–75.
26. John 13:37; 18:10.
27. John 21:15.
28. Matthew 26:33.
29. Revelation 1:10.
30. John 16:8–9.
31. Romans 1:20.
32. Matthew 2:1–12.
33. Acts 10.
34. 1 Samuel 3:9.

35. Psalm 23:6 KJV.

Chapter 5: Life in Concert

1. The term "beloved community" was first coined by Josiah Royce, founder of the Fellowship of Reconciliation. Martin Luther King Jr. popularized the term. See "Welcome to The Beloved Community," *www.thekingcenter.org/prog/bc/index. html.*

2. James M. Washington, ed., *A Testament of Hope: The Essential Writings and Speeches of Martin Luther King Jr.* (San Francisco: HarperSanFrancisco, 1986), 257.

3. Martin Luther King Jr., *Strength to Love* (Minneapolis: Fortress, 1981), 37.

4. The King Center has compiled King's teaching on the "beloved community" into a summary; go to *www.thekingcenter. org/prog/bc/index.html.* These quotes can be found there.

5. Matthew 5:39.

6. John 17:20–23, emphasis added.

7. Michael O. Emerson, *People of the Dream: Multiracial Congregations in the United States* (Princeton, N.J.: Princeton Univ. Press, 2006), 185.

8. Martin Luther King Jr., "Letter from Birmingham Jail," *www. thekingcenter.org/prog/non/letter.pdf.*

9. Ephesians 1:5–6; Galatians 3:26; 4:6–7; Romans 8:14–17.

10. Romans 8:17, 29; Colossians 1:15–20.

11. John 13:34–35.

12. Matthew 22:39.

13. Ephesians 2:11–22.

14. Revelation 5:9; 7:9; 11:9; 13:7; 14:6.

15. Chris Rice, "An Unrealized Dream: Billy Graham and Martin Luther King: The Road Not Traveled," *Sojourners*, January-February 1998, *www.calltorenewal.com/index.cfm?action= magazine.article&issue=soj9801&article=980141e.*

16. Ephesians 4:5.

17. Exodus 3:6, 15, 16; 4:5.

18. John 1:14.

19. Acts 6:3.

20. Acts 6:8.

21. Acts 7:56.

22. Matthew 25:21.

23. Paul F. Berliner, *Thinking in Jazz: The Infinite Art of Improvisation* (Chicago: Univ. of Chicago Press, 1994); see esp. chap. 2: "Hangin' Out and Jammin': The Jazz Community as an Educational System."

24. 1 Samuel 19:20.

25. Berliner, *Thinking in Jazz*, 41.

26. Luke 4:42.

27. Luke 5:16.

28. Luke 6:12.

29. Luke 11:1.

30. Bill Crow, *Jazz Anecdotes: Second Time Around* (New York: Oxford Univ. Press, 2005), 64.

31. John 17:21.

Chapter 6: Finding Your Voice

1. Jesus' brother James has something to say about this (James 2:14–19).

2. Quoted in Ken Burns, *Jazz: A Film by Ken Burns* (ten episodes; PBS Home Video, 2001).

3. Carl Ellis, *Free at Last? The Gospel in the African-American Experience* (Downers Grove, Ill.: InterVarsity, 1996), 38. I read this book at least once a year. It is here that I was first awakened to the possibility of a jazz-shaped Christianity.

4. Matthew 13:18–23.

5. Exodus 3:14.

6. Exodus 16:15.

7. Leviticus 23:33–36.
8. Cheryl Baumbach has also written a small book called *15 Seconds with God*, which is a great example of how to improvise off the book of Proverbs. It has been meaningful to many. You can email her at 15secondswithGod@gmail.com to get a copy.
9. Jon Paul Cardenas, his wife, Priscilla, and daughter, Zoey, live in the Denver area. Jon Paul plays a mean bass and is a testimony to God's grace and love. Motorcycles have had a significant place in his life, though he now says, "Motorcycles have lost the importance they once had, and that lifestyle is only a memory to me. I now focus on and love serving my Lord, wife, daughter, and church and worshiping through music."
10. Luke 1:1–3.
11. Proverbs 6:6.
12. Philippians 3:12.

Chapter 7: Developing Your Ear

1. Peter Senge et al., *The Fifth Discipline Fieldbook* (New York: Doubleday, 1994), 3.
2. John 13:34.
3. Gerald May, *Addiction and Grace: Love and Spirituality in the Healing of Addictions* (San Francisco: HarperSanFrancisco, 1988), 2.
4. Isaiah 42:1–4; 49:1–6; 50:4–9; 52:13–53:12.
5. John 13:1.
6. These next few paragraphs are heavily influenced by the work of James Hunter, who has written two of the simplest, yet not at all simplistic, books on servant leadership. They are profound, and I highly recommend them: *The Servant: A Simple Story about the True Essence of Leadership* (New York: Crown Business, 1998); *The World's Most Powerful Leadership Principle: How to Become a Servant Leader* (Colorado Springs: WaterBrook, 2004).

7. James 1:19.

8. John 20:14.

9. John 20:26.

10. John 21:4.

11. Luke 24:15–16.

12. Philippians 4:5.

13. 1 Corinthians 15:3–8.

14. John 16:7.

15. 1 Thessalonians 5:17.

16. Brad Braxton's term in *No Longer Slaves: Galatians and African American Experience* (Collegeville, Minn.: Liturgical Press, 2002), 5.

17. Os Guinness, *Prophetic Untimeliness* (Grand Rapids: Baker, 2003), 11.

18. Quoted in John F. Szwed, *Jazz 101: A Complete Guide to Learning and Loving Jazz* (New York: Hyperion, 2000), 33.

19. John 10:4–5.

20. John 16:8–11.

21. 1 Samuel 3:7.

22. 1 Samuel 3:8–10.

23. Dallas Willard, *In Search of Guidance: Developing a Conversational Relationship with God* (San Francisco: HarperSanFrancisco, 1993), 112.

24. John 10:37.

25. John 14:31.

26. Matthew 26:53.

27. John 16:23.

28. For a more detailed chronology and exegesis of the Dream speech, be sure to read Drew Hansen's book *The Dream: Martin Luther King Jr. and the Speech That Inspired a Nation* (New York: HarperCollins, 2003), in which he places the prepared speech and the delivered speech side by side.

Chapter 8: Singing the Blues

1. See Matthew 13:12.
2. Quoted in Elizabeth Goldson, ed., *Seeing Jazz* (San Francisco: Chronicle, 1997), 9.
3. James Cone, *The Spirituals and the Blues* (Maryknoll, N.Y.: Orbis, 1972), 103.
4. Ralph Ellison, *Invisible Man* (New York: Vintage, 1990), 8.
5. Biologists have wondered about and poets have pondered this question. The question was so intriguing that Maya Angelou sought to answer it in her autobiographical narrative *I Know Why the Caged Bird Sings*.
6. Quoted in Kent Hughes, *Are Evangelicals Born Again? The Character Traits of True Faith* (Wheaton, Ill.: Crossway, 1995), 96–97.
7. Mark Danner, *The Massacre at El Mozote* (New York: Vintage, 1994), 78–79.
8. Acts 16:16–40.
9. Cited in Charles Marsh, *God's Long Summer: Stories of Faith and Civil Rights* (Princeton, N.J.: Princeton Univ. Press, 1997), 21–22.
10. Mark 14:26.
11. Matthew 27:46. Jesus is quoting from Psalm 22:1.
12. Ralph Ellison, *Shadow and Act* (New York: Random House, 1964), 78.
13. Cornel West uses this phrase often in *Democracy Matters: Winning the Fight Against Imperialism* (New York: Penguin, 2004).
14. Romans 1:16.
15. 1 Corinthians 1:23.
16. John 6:61–66.
17. John 6:33, 35.
18. John 6:51.
19. John 6:53–56.

20. Romans 7:15, 24.
21. Colossians 1:27.
22. "Let us fix our eyes on Jesus, the author and perfecter of our faith, who for the joy set before him endured the cross, scorning its shame, and sat down at the right hand of the throne of God" (Hebrews 12:2).
23. 2 Samuel 11.
24. 2 Samuel 12:7.
25. Judges 16.
26. Loren Schoenberg, *The NPR Curious Listener's Guide to Jazz* (New York: Berkley, 2002), 12.
27. Mark 4:35–41.
28. Mark 5:1–20.
29. Matthew 4:23; 9:35.
30. Mark 16:15.
31. Luke 4:16–21.
32. Vinay Samuel and Chris Sugden, eds., *Mission as Transformation: A Theology of the Whole Gospel* (Irvine, Calif.: Regnum, 1999), 237.
33. If you have never fully grasped God's overwhelming concern for the poor and marginalized, take a few moments and ponder the following Scriptures: Isaiah 58; Jeremiah 9; 22; Ezekiel 16.
34. Matthew 11:4–6.
35. James H. Cone, *God of the Oppressed* (San Francisco: HarperSanFrancisco, 1975), 133.
36. Ibid., 108.
37. Ibid., 115–32.
38. Revelation 1:14–15.
39. Matthew 25:35–36, 40.
40. Cone, *God of the Oppressed*, 135.

Chapter 9: So What

1. Eric Nisenson, *The Making of* Kind of Blue*: Miles Davis and His Masterpiece* (New York: St. Martin's, 2000), 1.
2. Ibid.
3. If you do not own *Kind of Blue*, you might want to purchase it along with an album that is pre–*Kind of Blue*, perhaps some big band jazz, so you can hear the stark contrast.
4. See Jerry DeMuth, "Tired of Being Sick and Tired," *The Nation* 198 (June 1, 1964): 548–51.
5. See Nisenson, *Making of* Kind of Blue, 8–9.
6. Ibid., ix.
7. Mark 1:15.
8. Matthew 4:17.
9. Louis Armstrong, spoken introduction to "What a Wonderful World" (1970 version, Flying Dutchman).
10. "These men who have caused trouble all over the world have now come here" (Acts 17:6). The Greek word translated in the NIV as "cause trouble" can also be translated as "turn upside down."
11. Acts 4:34.
12. Philippians 4:22.

Share Your Thoughts

With the Author: Your comments will be forwarded to
the author when you send them to *zauthor@zondervan.com*.

With Zondervan: Submit your review of this book
by writing to *zreview@zondervan.com*.

Free Online Resources at
www.zondervan.com/hello

Zondervan AuthorTracker: Be notified whenever your
favorite authors publish new books, go on tour, or post
an update about what's happening in their lives.

Daily Bible Verses and Devotions: Enrich your life
with daily Bible verses or devotions that help you start
every morning focused on God.

Free Email Publications: Sign up for newsletters on
fiction, Christian living, church ministry, parenting, and
more.

Zondervan Bible Search: Find and compare
Bible passages in a variety of translations at
www.zondervanbiblesearch.com.

Other Benefits: Register yourself to receive online
benefits like coupons and special offers, or to participate
in research.

ZONDERVAN®
.com